The Inner
Revolution

David F. Olson

The Inner Revolution

**A theology for people
who don't understand theology**

JUDSON PRESS
VALLEY FORGE

First published 1973
by the Lutterworth Press, Luke House,
Farnham Road, Guildford, Surrey

Also published in 1973 by
Judson Press, Valley Forge, Pennsylvania

ACKNOWLEDGMENT

I would like to thank my wife Gun for the hours and effort spent
criticizing, questioning, commenting and correcting not only the Swedish
edition of this book but also the English. And even greater thanks for
her love and understanding when, in spite of my physical presence, I
have been far away in my thoughts.

Library of Congress Cataloging in Publication Data

Olson, David F   1938-   74-9498
    The inner revolution.

    1.   Youth—Religious Life.   1.   Title.
BV4539.S90413   248'.83   73-3088
ISBN 0-8170-0604-4
English translation © 1973 Lutterworth Press

Printed in Great Britain

Contents

Who had the knife?

Pete is on his way to the computer centre. He's going to get married. He isn't engaged. As a matter of fact, he isn't even going with anyone. But that doesn't make any difference because at the centre they have a brand new computer. Pete walks up to the computer and stuffs in his IBM card. He pushes a button with the word 'marriage' printed on it. Almost immediately he gets back his card together with another card. On the second card is the name, address and telephone number of a girl in the area who, according to the computer, would be the best wife for him. Pete goes to a telephone at the centre and rings her up. He arranges to meet her on Friday at four o'clock at the centre to fill in the necessary computer cards. They are going to get married!

How would you like to have this kind of system? Most people think it sounds just awful—but why? This type of marriage system is logical, scientific, and completely objective. This system is the result of the very latest in technology and built upon the things we value highest in society. But we don't like this kind of set-up because we feel that those things that really mean most to us don't have to do with technology, logic, and science, but with our feelings. We don't want to get married via the decision of some cold, objective computer. We want to experience something unscientific and illogical called 'falling in love'. We want this because we know that those things that meet us on the level of our feelings and not just in our logical minds are the most important things we can experience as human beings.

Remember what you have just read as you read this book. It is about the Christian Faith. The Christian Faith is not just knowledge but also love, humility, and inner peace. People are not tape-recorders on to which can be played what they should think and do. People have feelings. If the Christian Faith is going to touch and change people, then it is obvious that it must touch their feelings.

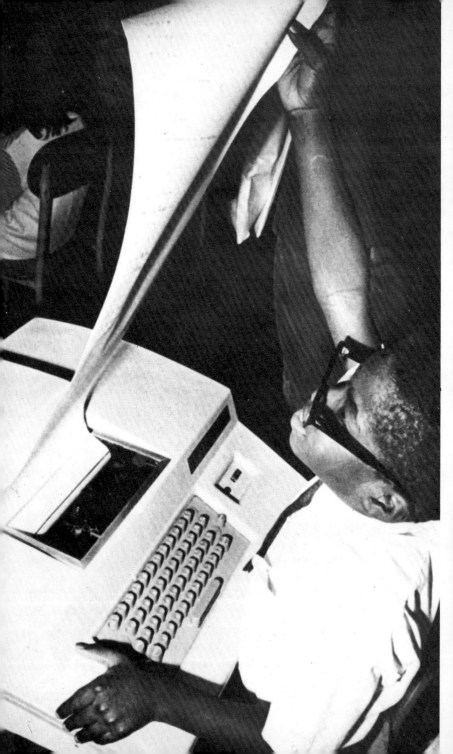

Perhaps you object to this and say: 'Yes, all this is well and good. But a person can't be steered just by feelings. A person must know and understand things;' which is true. And Christianity is not just feelings. But let me show you something.

A number of years ago some sociologists made an experiment. They showed a picture of a white man and a black man to some children and young people. The white man had a knife in his hand. The picture was shown for just a few seconds. Then those who had seen the picture were asked what they had seen. The children, who were aged six and seven, answered, 'A white man and a black.'

When they were asked who had the knife they almost all said that the white man had it.

But when they showed this same picture to white teenagers in an area where racial tension was very high, a strange thing happened. They too answered that they had seen a white man and a black man. But when asked who had the knife, most of them answered: 'The black'!

Did they lie?

No, they actually *saw* the knife in the hand of the black man even though it was not there. Why? This happened because these teenagers had within them feelings of prejudice and even hate that the six and seven-year-olds hadn't yet developed.

Can you trust what your eyes see and your ears hear and your mind understands? Is it always the truth? Or isn't it often the case that you see, hear, and understand only what you *want* to see, hear, and understand. It depends to a very great extent on your feelings.

That is why you must come to Christianity not only with your head, but also with your heart.

For discussion

1. What would be the advantages and disadvantages of getting married like Pete?
2. What prejudices or feelings do you have that could cause you to make the same kind of mistake as the white teenagers made over the knife? Who would you gang up on for instance and why?
3. Why do you think this book is called 'The Inner Revolution' and carries the picture it has on the front?

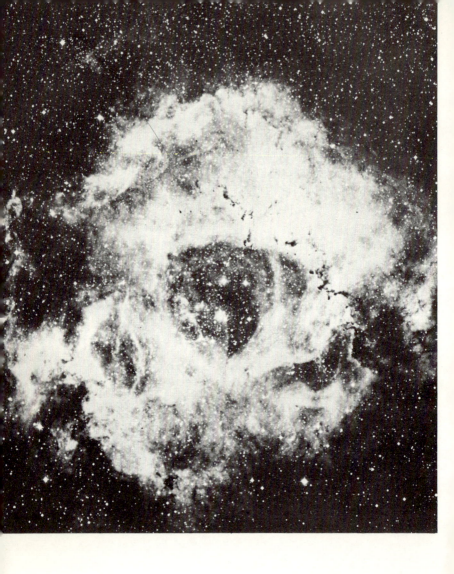

Nebula photographed
through the Schmidt
telescope at the Mount
Palomar observatory in
California.

The universe and I

About the God of Mr. Average

Almost every day we read in the paper or see on television that something new has been discovered. Man has always been an inquisitive creature. With the aid of fantastic new tools, he has discovered the inside of atoms, studied the sex life of bacteria, and landed on the moon. Most scientists have been overwhelmed by this great adventure. Their discoveries seem unbelievable. Many feel a deep sense of humility as a result of their research and discoveries. They know that for every question answered, ten new ones appear. They feel small because they know so little.

It might seem that all people would feel this same sense of smallness which is felt by scientists. But that is not the case. Mr. Average (who actually has very little to do with research) often feels big and proud. He is not impressed with what is discovered but with the *discoverer*. He is impressed with man, not nature. And since Mr. Average is a man, he is rather impressed with himself—even though he really doesn't know much at all. The universe, nature and everything else in creation is rather small. He, as a member of the human race, is huge.

Let's imagine for a moment that you get an assignment in school. You are to build a model of the universe—the earth, moon, sun and stars. You are to make it a scale model. The earth is to be ½ inch in diameter instead of 8,000 miles (a scale of 1:1,000,000,000). You are to reduce everything in this scale model universe, both in size and distance, to the same extent as you have reduced the size of the earth. First you hang the earth up on a thread in the middle of your room. You are now going to hang up the moon, sun, the star nearest the earth, the north star and the star farthest away. But you have a problem. If the model is to be a scale model, how far away from the earth should you hang them? What do you think? Write down what you think are the right answers:

The moon ....
The sun ....
The nearest star ....
The north star ....
The farthest known star ....
The answers are on the next page.

How did you make out? You probably did like most people and guessed quite wrongly. Now you can understand what I mean when I said that the universe and the rest of creation are not at all as impressive and great for most people as they really are.

This is interesting but you may wonder what all this has to do with Christianity. If most people believe the universe or creation to be much smaller than it actually is, then God or the Creator they believe in (or don't believe in) is also much smaller than he actually is. This is a big problem for many people concerning their belief in God. Their God is too small. He is much more like a kind of Santa Claus than what Christianity understands by the word *God*. God has become so small, and man so big, that Mr. Average has a hard time in believing in God any more.

I understand Mr. Average. But he doesn't know very much about the God Christianity is concerned with. The God with whom this book deals is not a small God who can do nothing. He is the Creator. He has created the universe, the atoms, life, everything. And he keeps this creation in order and harmony.

It is of this God that the prophet Isaiah wrote,

Behold, the Lord God comes with might, and his arm rules for him;...Who has measured the waters in the hollow of his hand and marked off the heavens with a span, enclosed the dust of the earth in a measure and weighed the mountains in scales and the hills in a balance? Who has directed the Spirit of the Lord, or as his counsellor has instructed him? Whom did he consult for his enlightenment, and who taught him the path of justice, and taught him knowledge, and showed him the way of understanding? Behold, the nations are like a drop from a bucket, and are accounted as the dust on the scales; behold, he takes up the isles like fine dust. . . . To whom then will you liken God or what likeness compare with him?

Isaiah 40: 10, 12–15, 18 (RSV)

For discussion

1. When the Russian cosmonaut Yuri Gagarin returned to earth after the first manned space flight, he said: 'God does not exist. I didn't see him up there.' If you had had a chance to speak with Gagarin what would you have said?
2. Give someone you know a test on their knowledge of the size of the universe using the scale model on page 11. How did they guess?

Answers

The Moon 15 inches, the sun 500 feet, the nearest star 19,000 miles, the north star 70,000 miles, the star farthest away that we know of (Qasar 16) 47,000,000,000,000 miles.

How can God have such long legs?

Many people believe that science and religion are in conflict with one another and that one must somehow choose between them. They know that there is a great difference between how long it took to create the earth according to science and that which is written in the Bible in the book of Genesis. The problem is that people mix together the role of religion and the role of science. If you read the Bible as if it were science you are going to get into trouble. And if you come to science for answers to your religious questions you are also going to get into trouble. Science and religion attempt to answer different questions. Science wants to answer the questions: *When* was everything created? *What* was created? *How* did it happen? and *Where*? Religion seeks answers to questions such as: *Who* created? *What is the meaning* of my life? *How shall I live*?

If both science and religion respect one another and one another's roles, they can get along fine together and even help one another. We have already seen how it is easier to get an idea of what Christianity means with *God* as Creator by listening to what science can tell us about creation.

Dr. Charles Towens, winner of the Nobel Prize in Physics, wrote once:

> To me science and religion are both universal and basically very similar. . . . The goal of science is to discover the order in the universe, and to understand through it the things we sense around us, and even man himself. . . . The goal of religion may be stated, I believe, as an understanding (and hence acceptance) of the purpose and meaning of our universe and how we fit into it. . . . Understanding the *order* in the universe and understanding the *purpose* in the universe are not identical, but they are also not very far apart.

Much of what Christianity teaches seems unbelievable and impossible. But when we take a closer look at what science says is possible and impossible, then it becomes easier for us to believe. It has always been difficult for people to understand how God can be from eternity to eternity—without beginning and without end. They ask, 'How can God be invisible?' A child in Sunday school asked once, 'How can God have such long legs that he can stand on earth and be in heaven at the same time?' What this child was asking was, 'How can God be everywhere at once?'

Let's look at some 'impossible' and 'unbelievable' things which are nevertheless true, in order to help you understand that much more is possible than you think.

Come along on a fantastic trip!

I would like you to come along on a space trip to a star called Arkturus. It is thirty–three light years away from our earth. (A light year is the distance light travels in one year at a speed of 186,284 miles per second.) You are to travel at just under the speed of light. Let us say, 186,000 miles per second. Your trip begins tomorrow at eight in the morning.

You arrive at Arkturus, judging from your clock and the empty feeling in your stomach, at about noon the same day. During the time your spaceship is making the turn for the return trip, you eat what you have taken along with you. You arrive home again at about six in the evening. You jump out of your spaceship and run over to one of your friends who lives near by, to tell him about your journey. You ring the door-bell and an old man whom you don't recognize answers the door. You ask for Henry and he answers: '*I* am Henry'. During your trip your friend has become sixty six years older. You are only a half day older and yet it took you sixty six years to make the trip to Arkturus and back. How can this be? The answer is that at the speed of light, time stops. Time had almost stopped completely for you since you travelled at almost the speed of light. Unbelievable you say!

But this is not all that happens at the speed of light. If you had increased your speed a little in your spaceship and actually reached the speed of light, then several other unbelievable things would have happened to you. In one way you would have disappeared, and in another you would have become as large as the universe! All this sounds completely impossible, but scientists say that it is, in fact, what would happen if it were possible to reach the speed of light. And some of these things are exactly the kind of things many say are impossible for God—he who, according to Christianity, created everything in the first place.

What science discovers about our universe does not make it more difficult to believe but often much easier. And scientists can learn from religion that they were not the first to speak of such unbelievable things. Centuries before Christ a Psalmist said,

> Lord, thou hast been our dwelling place in all generations. Before the mountains were brought forth, or ever thou hadst formed the earth and the world, from everlasting to everlasting thou art God. Thou turnest man back to the dust, and sayest, 'Turn back, O children of men!' For a thousand years in thy sight are but as yesterday when it is past, or as a watch in the night. Thou dost sweep men away; they are like a dream . . .

Psalm 90: 1–5 (RSV)

For discussion

1. On page 14 we read that some questions belong to science to answer and others belong to religion. Do the questions asked in Isaiah 40: 10, 12–15, 18 (pages 12-13) belong to science or religion?
2. How would you answer the child on page 15?
3. Tell someone you know what would happen to you if you made a trip to Arkturus as described on page 15. What was their reaction?

Why does a snowflake always have six arms?

Much of what has been said in the last chapters is perhaps news to you. It is not easy to imagine the greatness of the universe. Neither is it easy to fathom timelessness—without beginning or end. But you don't have to turn to the universe or measure the speed of light to discover the Creator's work. All you have to do is to look around you and you will discover miracles. And they are all part of the one miracle of *order* and *harmony*. Everywhere you look you will see that things are built according to a system of order and harmony. Almost everyone has seen a snowflake. But did you know that a snowflake always has six arms? How can this be? Do you know that quartz crystals always have six sides? It makes no difference if a crystal comes from India, Brazil or Sweden—they all have six sides.

Everything, from atoms to stars, function according to a definite system of order. This same miracle of order is discovered by both microscope and telescope.

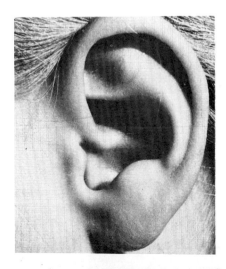

Quartz crystals, Stråssa,
Sweden.

Do you know that in your head you have a combination radio, tape-recorder, and stereo unit? It is much smaller than the smallest transistor radio and of much higher quality. It can play ten tones between each tone played on a piano or 1,500 tones in all. It has 24,000 strings. And the whole unit functions automatically. You can play in a melody automatically and save it in your tape library and play it back whenever you want to. This fantastic instrument is your ears. Where did you get them? You say: 'Mum made them in just nine months.' What a mother you must have! She must be a fantastic engineer!

Do you know that you also have two video-cameras which work completely automatically? They can make the correct adjustments in a fraction of a second. They can adjust not only the amount of light entering the camera, but also the *distance*! You can 'set up' this camera, film, process and record these films in your film library in a fraction of a second. You say that your mother made these instruments in only nine months! What a mother!

There are many miracles that we can see around us or within us if only we look. And we always find a system, an order, a harmony. Science could never make any progress if this order or harmony did not exist.

How can we describe the Creator of such a universe? Which word should we use when we speak of the God who has created a universe

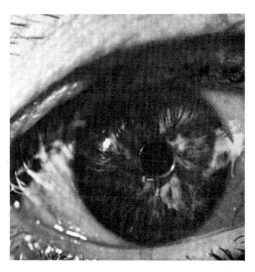

which our minds cannot even imagine—a universe built upon unity and perfection? Christianity uses the word Holy. God is holy. We sing a hymn which begins Holy, Holy, Holy, Lord God Almighty.

The first Article of the Creed is, 'I believe in God the father almighty, maker of heaven and earth.'

For discussion

1. Where in our church services do we speak of God as holy?
2. The Danish philosopher Sören Kierkegaard wrote once, 'God does not exist. He is eternal!' What do you think he meant?

Destruction or Progress? On the *left* a Polaris being shot up from a submarine. Its warhead has the same destructive power as all the bombs and shells used in World War II. On the *right* a weather satellite being sent up from Cape Kennedy—in the service of mankind.

In the mirror . . . chaos and disorder

But not everything is order and perfection. When we move our attention from the order and harmony of nature and a holy God, to people, we are in for a shock. When we look at ourselves as human beings, we can hardly say that all is harmony. As a matter of fact, we would have to admit that it is just the opposite. Man creates chaos and disorder. We live in an age of unrest, hate, fear and even terror.

The word 'terror' describes our situation very well. Many believe that the only thing that has saved the world from stumbling into a third world war is that there exists something called 'the balance of terror'. Russia and the USA have so many rockets, planes, and atomic weapons that both sides understand that he who starts the third world war also commits suicide. It has been calculated that there are enough atomic weapons today to wipe out all the people on earth *six times*. A world teetering on the edge of atomic war; a world in which a small percentage lives in luxury and the majority lives in the shadow of starvation, and a world in which violence is widespread is hardly a pretty and harmonious place to look at.

Did you know that there are only three creatures that make war? Ants, rats, and man. But it is only man who freely chooses to make war. A wolf hunts and kills for food. This belongs to the order of nature. But man doesn't kill because he's hungry: he kills because he hates. It seems to many that a cannibal is the most uncivilized of all men. But is it more civilized to shoot down thousands of people because they are hated or because they represent the 'wrong' political opinion, 'wrong' country or 'wrong' race? Man is one of the very few creatures who kills creatures of his own kind—his fellow men. When animals of the same kind fight, it is similar to Indian wrestling. When men fight they are literally 'dead serious'.

What are we going to do about all this? How can we reduce hate, division, war, and unrest in the world? We *must* find solutions if we are to continue living on this planet we call earth. The chaos and disorder that rule the world must be reduced.

Many believe that education will solve the problem. Education is of unbelievable importance, but it is not a patent solution. We only have to look at our own century to discover that it was precisely among the educated and so-called civilized countries that the greatest wars and tragedies occurred. Verdun, Dresden, Auschwitz, Hiroshima are not names of primitive tribes or places in darkest Africa, but the names of places in the developed, civilized and educated world where some of this century's greatest tragedies took place.

Someone has said that 'knowledge of a problem is fifty per cent of the problem's solution'. This is so. We *must* have as much and as excellent an education as is possible. Education and knowledge are without a doubt fifty per cent of the solution to the problems of this world. But the other fifty per cent? How are we to reach the hearts and wills of people to motivate and stimulate them to *use* the solutions they have found in knowledge and education?

People are not tape-recorders. They have wills and feelings, which determine whether they use their knowledge for good or evil—or not at all.

Nowadays, not surprisingly, we turn to technology for solutions to our problems. Technology can do miracles at times. But it can also give us the very tools we use to destroy all higher developed life on this earth. It all depends on *how* technology is used. Just a little more than one hundred years ago, a soldier could shoot about two shots a minute with his primitive rifle. Today with the aid of technology, he can shoot at a rate of 6,000 per minute.

We must be very careful in our admiration of what technology can achieve. When we realize what miracles and services technology could do for us, it makes you want to cry when you discover that the money spent on military equipment in a year is greater than the *combined* national incomes of Asia, Africa and Latin America. John F. Kennedy said, 'For the first time in history we have the means to give food to all. We lack only the will.'

It is popular nowadays to believe that material well-being will solve all the world's problems. Many believe that if all peoples of the world had a high and just standard of living, then war, division and hate would disappear of themselves. Unfortunately, it isn't that simple.

There is no evidence for this belief. We must, of course, work for a more just distribution of the wealth of the world. Present starvation and injustice demand this. These conditions are, without a doubt, the cause of much of the division and unrest in the world. But don't expect a high standard of living to solve all problems because it won't. If this were the case, then many of the countries in the world today with high standards of living would be show-cases of happiness and well-being, where loneliness and suicide were rare occurrences. But just the opposite is often the case. Jesus was right when he said, 'Man does not live by bread alone'. People have other deep needs which must also be taken into account.

Lords of Creation
Paul Weber

For discussion

1. Why do you think this chapter is called 'In the mirror . . . chaos and disorder'?
2. What do you think the picture on page 21 will say?
3. What on page 24 could explain the shock on the animals' faces?
4. Is technological progress good or bad? What do you think?

The greatest tragedy

The tragedy of man is not only that he is aggressive, hates, and makes war but that it is possible for him to do precisely the opposite—and he refuses to. We are failures not just because we do evil but also much more because we fail to do good.

We take for granted that since we have a better developed brain than, for example, an ape, this automatically means that we are somehow 'better' than an ape. But can we in all honesty say this? Are we automatically 'better' because we have received greater possibilities to think, learn and create? Doesn't 'betterness' also depend on *what we do* with the possibilities we have received? Doesn't it also depend on *how* we use our brains and our ability to reason? In Genesis it says that man was created in the image of God. This does not mean that we look like God or that he looks like us. It means that we have received possibilities that no other creature has received. But to be a man, to be human, means to use those possibilities we have received, not just to boast that we have a higher developed brain. Christianity teaches that man is a 'sinner'. To sin means to 'miss the target'—to miss the possibilities we have as human beings.

Someone has said that 'To say that monkeys are almost as good as man is to insult monkeys'.

Perhaps the best evidence of this is an experiment made a number of years ago.

Several monkeys were placed in cages. One monkey, in a cage by himself, could look at the other monkeys in a neighbouring cage through a window made of one-way glass. He could see the other monkeys but they couldn't see him. The monkey that was alone had learned to pull a chain each time he was hungry and needed food. The people conducting the experiment built the second cage with electrical wires on the floor, so that each time the single monkey pulled the chain for food the other monkeys received an unpleasant shock.

26

This monkey therefore could see his 'fellow-monkeys' twist and turn in pain each time he needed food, but when he related pulling the chain to the pain experienced by the other monkeys he stopped pulling the chain. This was so with twelve out of fifteen monkeys tested. These monkeys would rather go without food than cause pain to their fellow monkeys. Can as much be said of humans?

The greatest tragedy of all is that human beings have so many more possibilities than monkeys. We are sinners, not only because we hate, but above all else because we have the possibility of loving or forgiving and we refuse to do either. Fights between monkeys come as an automatic response to their instinct for survival. Fights among men come because they reject their possibilities of creating harmony.

Instead of building . . .	we destroy.
Instead of loving . . .	we hate.
Instead of learning from our mistakes . . .	we make the same mistake over and over again.
Instead of forgiving . . .	we promise never to forget.

You do something stupid at home. You say something to your father which hurts him terribly. You know it hurts—that's why you said it. You wanted to hurt him. The next day you also know that you have a *creative possibility*. All you have to do is say one word and everything will be all right. All you have to say is 'sorry' or 'forgive me' and he will surely forgive you—but you refuse. Why? You don't *want* to. You have the power to create harmony, but you refuse.

We humans have missed the target so completely that all over the world men have had to create an artificial system of order simply to survive. This artificial system of order is called 'the law'. The law exists for us as a guide-line, but also to *force* men to deal justly with one another. Imagine how much better it would be if we didn't miss the target, if we really lived up to our possibilities as human beings! How much cheaper it would be, and less trouble! We wouldn't need policemen, prisons, defence, or even the keys in our pockets. We wouldn't have to lock anything up.

For discussion

1. What possibilities does man have that animals lack?
2. What is sin?
3. Read Matthew 25:14–30. Why was the Master angry with the last servant? Had the servant perhaps stolen the money or spent it on 'wine, women and song'?
4. Someone has said that 'The opposite of love is not hate but apathy'. What does this mean?
5. Of which possibilities is man the worst steward?

The problem inside . . . our inner chaos

Why don't people live up to their possibilities? Why do they choose what is wrong and destructive? There are many reasons. But one of the really important ones is that people as individuals experience a kind of inner chaos or disorder which cripples them. To this inner chaos belong such things as feelings of guilt, feeling unloved, fear of death, loneliness and a sense of meaninglessness.

Think back a moment to the last time you were really unkind or stupid towards someone! Most of us don't have to think back so very far. Didn't you have a feeling inside that said, 'Now why did I do that'? This feeling is called a guilt feeling. It comes often when we have been mean or stupid towards someone or towards ourselves. We get this feeling for several reasons. Firstly, because we have hurt someone. Secondly, because we have further isolated ourselves from precisely those fellow human beings we need so much. And lastly, because we know that we have done exactly the opposite of what we had it in us to do. Unrest, division and loneliness have been created by us instead of harmony and peace. Why do we do it?

Loneliness is one of the greatest problems of today, and it is not just the fault of 'the modern age' or society. We all create and keep loneliness alive deliberately. We do this when we do things that separate us from others and when we refuse to ask for forgiveness.

We cannot tolerate loneliness. We become bitter and unreal. Some would rather die than live in loneliness. A study of suicides in America showed that many who committed suicide had moved about a great deal during the last months of their lives, but had not succeeded anywhere in making contact with other people. Even though these people were surrounded by others they still felt lonely and unloved.

Do humans experience a greater need than the need to be loved? Without the security that love creates, people get into all kinds of difficulties. We know that children who never experience love are hurt for life. And adults have the very same need of love.

Another part of our inner chaos is our fear of death. Many people, probably most people, are afraid of death. Why do you think we are afraid to die? Why do you think that people are even afraid to *talk* about or discuss death? It's not because it will be painful to die. Many experience their last moments as peaceful and relaxed. We are afraid to die because we don't want to be a *nothing*. We are afraid of not *being* anything anymore. We can put it this way: We are afraid that we won't be at our own funeral. Life has meaning for us only when we are 'there'. Death will fix things so that we aren't 'there' any more. Then life, then 'I' will be without meaning. It seems so meaningless that 'I' who exist today should someday not be 'there'.

A feeling of meaninglessness is very common today especially among young people. It is another part of our inner chaos. We don't talk much about this feeling but it has a great deal to do with how we live, what we think is important in life, and what kind of people we are. In the past there was a meaning to life. It was simply to survive. This was a poor meaning—but it worked. Today many have a high standard of living, financial security, and survival guaranteed by a welfare system. The old meaning of life as mere survival has disappeared. It was not intended that a welfare system or a high standard of living should create meaninglessness. It just worked out that way. Welfare, security and a high standard of living are good. They open the door to a higher and better meaning to life than mere survival. But we must make the most of these possibilities.

For discussion

1. What did Jesus mean when he said, 'Man does not live by bread alone'?
2. Where in the church service do we speak of the chaos we create?
3. Is loneliness (a) not having any friends (b) something felt even when surrounded by friends (c) having an opinion that is not popular? Which type of loneliness do you think is the most common? Which type have you personally felt—or never felt?

How our inner chaos cripples us

We have spoken of the inner chaos experienced by an individual, of guilt, loneliness, feeling unloved, fear of death, and a sense of meaninglessness. What happens when a person lives daily with this chaos? Some run, some create even more problems and disorder, some just can't bear the load and break down. Few come close to living up to their possibilities.

Alcohol

People try often to hide from their problems. Many use alcohol for this purpose, because alcohol deadens the senses. Everything becomes cloudy and unclear. I have heard people say 'Only when I am drunk can I forget my problems', or, 'The only time I am really happy is when I have had a few drinks'.

If problems *really* did disappear, then getting drunk would be a great idea. But problems don't disappear. To flee and hide behind a curtain of drunkenness is no solution. We become sober and have to return to our problems. All our misery is still there and probably is even worse. Perhaps our salary has been used up. Perhaps things have been said in drunkenness that have hurt others. The result is only more loneliness, isolation, and meaninglessness. Why can't people be happy *without* a drink or two? That is the question to which we need to find an answer.

Drugs

Many people try to change things with drugs. For a very short time everything that is black and chaotic becomes light, warm, and exciting. But this feeling soon disappears and is replaced by the need for more (and often stronger) drugs, and more exciting escapes from reality. We

must see life as it is. The world is full of loneliness, hate, injustice and meaninglessness but, no matter how many warm, lovely and exciting experiences we have, feeling high on drugs *doesn't change one single thing*. Things just get worse.

Suicide

The most tragic attempt to flee chaos in desperation is suicide. A person chooses the chaos of death instead of the chaos of life. In most cases those who attempt suicide don't really want to die. An attempt at suicide is often a last desperate cry for love. It is a cry not only with words, but with life itself.

Mental breakdown

A mental breakdown may be another way of adjusting to, reacting to, or escaping from, life's disharmony. Breakdowns are very common and express themselves in many different ways. Sometimes a person sinks into deep depression. Sometimes an abnormal life-style is developed since a so-called normal life-style just doesn't work. Sometimes a person leaves the unpleasantness of this world and seeks, as it were, another world within or beyond himself. Sometimes one's senses just turn off automatically when reality becomes too painful. This is like shock in the case of physical injury. Often a person is helped or cured by simply establishing some kind of contact with someone to whom he can talk openly. This someone can be a friend, a minister, a doctor or a therapist. Sometimes a person needs medical attention or medicine to decrease or to take away depression.

For discussion

Alcohol and drugs should be (a) forbidden (b) freely available (c) available as they are now. What do you think?

The 'normal' person and his chaos

What about the so-called 'normal' person and the chaos he faces in life? Most don't drink too much, take drugs, try to commit suicide or experience a breakdown. What about these 'normal' people?

Even if a person is what many would call 'normal' he is still affected and crippled by disharmony in his life. We know that most people at times experience feelings of unrest and stress. This feeling may express itself in the form of an ulcer, headaches, general tiredness, or the 'blues'. People don't talk much about their inner unrest—but they do take plenty of pills for it. Often people feel afraid to speak of their inner problems because they are afraid that others will not consider them 'normal'. Some feel that it is not right to complain. The American philosopher Henry David Thoreau wrote that 'most people live lives of quiet desperation'. We feel deep unrest but don't want to talk about the possible causes. But even if we are silent about our desperation and actually succeed in presenting to the world a 'normal' front, our lives are still affected by this unrest.

Have you ever heard the phrases 'work addict' or 'he is married to his job'? These are descriptions of the way many 'normal' people literally offer their lives to their jobs. They don't always do it for the money or even for advancement. Sometimes they do it because they feel forced to do it. The effort, and even the drudgery, of a job can serve as a way of fleeing from the problems and troubles of life. If we are always busy then we never have time to think about life's disturbing realities. As burdensome as continual work may be, it can be much easier than, for example, facing our marriage problems at home. Vicktor Frankl, a famous psychiatrist in Austria, believes that today's stress and tempo have come about as a means of rushing us through life—always busy, with never a moment to think or meditate. Weekends and vacations can be sheer torture for people who use their jobs as a flight from reality or as life's only source of meaning. Psychia-

trists call this a 'Sunday-neurosis'. Imagine what a catastrophe retirement can be for such people.

Have you ever wondered why some people are always changing cars, boats, houses and other things? Even if the 'old' car is almost new, they just seem unable to stand it any more. Often it is because when these people buy a new car, they are not just buying a new *car*: they are also buying meaning for their lives. Bought meaning is sometimes the *only* meaning in a person's life. He spends a great deal of energy, time and worry keeping his job and earning more money. Family fights often centre on minor questions of money. The man of the house is often forced to 'moonlight' and the wife to work to achieve or maintain the standard the family feels it *must* have. All this creates unrest, division, loneliness and stress. There is an evil circle where chaos creates chaos.

Another way people react to the chaos they face is with just plain *egoism*. If a person doesn't experience love, forgiveness, and meaning in life, he often turns to egoism to help him feel that he *has something* or *is something*. He becomes proud and domineering, looks down upon others, wants power, and fights to win every argument. The results are, of course, more chaos, guilt, loneliness and meaninglessness. Even truth means nothing any more since an egoist is more interested in *who has* the truth than *what is* the truth.

There is an endless supply of reactions a person can experience in his attempts to cope with his inner disharmony. Generally these reactions cripple. There is seldom a 'normal' person who lives up to his potential or possibilities, so that all of us who experience crippling inner disharmony or chaos can find that Christianity will give 'God's peace which passes all understanding'. Peace is an old word from the Old Testament. It means order and harmony.

Is there anything people need more today than inner peace?

For discussion

1. Apart from earning money, what are some of the reasons why people work?
2. Freedom is very important: freedom to be ourselves, freedom to achieve our potential, freedom to seek for truth. From what you have just read, what are some of the things that make us unfree?

For I do not do what I want . . .

What do people do to get rid of the chaos and disharmony they face? For most people the answer is simply 'nothing'. It has always been the role of religion to deal with our inner life, but few people really take their religion seriously enough to get any help from it. Most have a sort of 'do-it-yourself' religion that sounds all right but doesn't really work. Their creed is something like, 'I believe in God the Father Almighty, Creator of heaven and earth. I believe in myself.' But if you look closely at this religion you will find that it is a sort of 'religion to escape all religions' and a fooling of oneself.

How many times have I heard someone say: 'The main thing is to live by the ten commandments or the sermon on the mount.' But when asked to repeat the ten commandments or say what the sermon on the mount is all about, they are forced to admit that they can't. Another very popular phrase is: 'The main thing is that we live as good a life as we can.' But how good is 'as good as we can'? Do people really consider what possibilities they have for doing good when they say this? Doesn't it generally work out that people live as they *want to* and when they don't want to 'do good' any more then 'to hell with it'? Or perhaps someone says, 'I'm as good as the next man.' But is the 'next man' anything to compare yourself with? Remember, he is saying the same thing about you!

Jesus didn't say: 'Be as good as you can' or 'be as good as the next man'. He said: 'You, therefore, must be perfect, as your heavenly Father is perfect.' We should compare ourselves with God's order and holiness. We should compare ourselves with what we could be and could do if we lived up to our potential. The point is that we who are created in the image of God, with possibilities that no other creature possesses, should love, build and create order and harmony, just as God did in his creation.

Christianity teaches that a 'do-it-yourself' religion just doesn't work.

We *know* how we should behave towards our fellow men. We know of meaningful things we could do. But we don't do what we should, anyway. We are like Paul who writes of himself:

> For I do not do the good I want, but the evil I do not want is what I do. . . . For I delight in the law of God in my inmost self, but I see in my members another law at war with the law of my mind and making me a captive to the law of sin which dwells in my members. Wretched man that I am! Who will deliver me from this body of death? Thanks be to God through Jesus Christ our Lord!
>
> Romans 7: 19, 22–25 (RSV)

But if there is a God, why doesn't he 'do something'?

Why doesn't God do something to stop the chaos created by man—war, for instance? This question is based on man's eternal search for an answer to the problem of evil, and why it exists. Let's look a bit closer.

In the first place we must remember that it isn't God but man who makes war and creates chaos. We human beings don't make war because we have to, as if God made us that way. As human beings we have enough brains, capabilities, and freedom to build a world of peace, well-being and justice—if we want to.

Why don't we want to? This is the central question. It is not for logical reasons that we refuse. It is because of fear, pride, and selfishness. It is because of deep feelings of disharmony and chaos. If there is to be a change then something must reach not only our heads, but also our hearts. A philosopher called Spinoza once said that 'the only thing that can change a feeling is not reason but another stronger feeling'. We must remember that when we ask God 'to do something' we are asking him to do something with and through us. We must ask him first to do something that reaches our hearts and changes both our feelings and wills.

The second thing to ask when we want God to do something is, 'Just what do we expect God to do anyway?' We should not ask God to do something that will destroy our freedom as human beings, for that would destroy *us* in the process.

Let me give you an example. A man has two sons whom he loves very much, but who are always fighting with one another. They don't love one another at all. If the father loves his sons he has got to *do something* to stop them from hurting or killing each other. But he doesn't do too much. He could take his sons to a doctor for an operation on their brains and thereby cut down their aggression. But he does not do this. To do so would mean a drastic change in their personalities. This would take from them a large part of their freedom or possibilities —part of their humanness. Therefore when God 'does something' it must be something that does not destroy our freedom. If he were to *force* us to love one another, this would no longer be love. If he took from us our freedom, we would no longer be human beings created in the image of God.

The central and most important belief in Christianity is the belief that God really 'does something'. This is exactly what Christianity is all about: God's action in Jesus Christ. John writes: 'For God so loved the world that he gave his only begotten son so that whosoever believeth in him shall not perish but have everlasting life. For God did not send his son into the world to condemn the world but that the world through him would be saved.'

When God acts in Christ he wants not only to reach our minds or our reason, but (most important of all) our emotions—through his love, suffering, forgiveness and our relationship with him. It is God's wish to liberate each man from himself—from his own crippling chaos. Jesus said, 'Peace I leave with you, my peace I give to you, not as the world gives it to you. Let not your hearts be troubled or afraid.'

But remember, and be thankful, that when God 'does something', he doesn't do too much. He *forces no one*. We are always free to answer 'yes' or 'no'. We are even free to accuse him of giving us freedom.

Second Article of the Creed

I believe in Jesus Christ His only Son, our Lord; who was conceived by the Holy Ghost, born of the virgin Mary; suffered under Pontius Pilate, was crucified dead and buried; He descended into hell; the third day he rose again from the dead; He ascended into heaven, and sitteth on the right hand of God the Father almighty; from thence he shall come to judge the quick and the dead.

For discussion

1. When evaluating a person which of the following do you think most people would regard as most important?
   (a) Intelligence (b) talent (c) looks (d) money (e) race (f) education (g) social class.

2. Often a moral aspect is used in evaluating people. What do you think most people regard as important? That one is (a) kind (b) just (c) honest (d) does his share?

3. In Luke 15: 11–32 we read a parable Jesus told to show how God evaluates people. Read it and consider the following questions:
   (a) What kind of reception would you receive if you did what the younger son did?
   (b) In what way had the younger son 'earned' his welcome?
   (c) What difference is there between how God evaluates a person and how people generally (the elder son, for instance) evaluate a person?

The story of the king and the flower girl

There was once a young king who ruled a small country. He lived in a big castle with his servants, but without a queen, for he was not married. Each week, as was the custom, he took a ride out into his kingdom to see that everything was in order.

One day, when he was on the way back to the castle, he happened to pass through the town square. There his eye was caught by a beautiful girl, who sold flowers at a stand. She was so beautiful that he could not forget her. The next day he decided that it would be a good idea to ride out and inspect the kingdom again instead of waiting for another week. He began to ride out every day and, of course, always managed to pass through the town square for a look at the flower girl.

After this had gone on for a month he knew he was in love with the girl and wanted to marry her. He called together his advisers and told them the good news. There was going to be a royal wedding. Everyone was very happy. But when he returned to his room a very disturbing thought struck him. What would happen if he ordered the girl to marry him but if she never fell in love with him? This thought troubled the king deeply. The most important thing to him was not that he acquired a queen but above all else that he got a *wife who loved him*. Could she ever forget that he was the king and she a mere flower girl? The young king tried to find a solution to the problem. He was so worried that he neither ate nor slept. After a few days he hit on a solution.

He would go to the flower girl in the square, in his gilded coach, drawn by six of his finest horses. Before him would march an orchestra, and behind him the finest regiment in his army. The carriage would then stop in front of the stand of the flower girl and a red rug would be rolled out to it. Then the king would walk to the stand, dressed in his finest clothes, and wearing his crown and royal jewels. She would surely be impressed. But after a while the king gave up this idea. It wasn't any good. She would, of course, be impressed. But to be impressed and to be in love are not the same thing.

The king had another idea. He would *give* to the flower girl the gilded coach with the six horses. He would give her a regiment of soldiers, an orchestra, jewels, money, the finest silks in the world. Surely she would be grateful? But after a day or two the king gave up this idea as well. It just wasn't right. Oh, yes, she would be grateful. But to be grateful, even eternally grateful, and to be in love are not the same thing.

At last the king came upon the only real solution. He would not go to the girl as a king, but disguised as a beggar or a farmer. He would go to her on her level and try to win her heart.

The next day, early in the morning, while it was still dark, the young king left the castle by the back way and made his way towards the town square. He was nervous and unsure. He who had power over the entire kingdom, power over the wealth and armies of the country, was suddenly powerless. There was one place were he did not have power and that was over the heart of the flower girl. There, freedom must rule. Freedom to love or to hate, freedom to say 'yes' or 'no'.

Did the king succeed with his plan? We don't know. He has made his move. Now it depends on the girl.

God comes to us as an ordinary human being, as a child named Jesus, born in a manger. He could have thought of a more impressive way to come to 'do something?' He could have come amongst exploding stars, with a moon that turned bright red, oceans that were transformed to gold and mountains to jewels. He could have come on a great stairway from the heavens, made from the light of the sun. We would certainly have been impressed, but to be impressed and to love are not the same thing.

Certainly God could have arranged for all mankind to become richer. Everyone would have a high standard of living. We would all be very grateful. But to be grateful and to experience the change in our hearts when we live in a personal relationship with God are not the same thing.

God chooses to come disguised as Jesus Christ. God, Creator of heaven and earth, with power over the universe, atoms and the miracle we call life, chooses *not* to use his power to rule our hearts. Does God succeed with his plan to come to us disguised as a man, as a child born in a manger? God has 'done something'. Now it depends on us.

For discussion

1. Find your own reasons why the king didn't have the girl arrested and force her to marry him?
2. In the parable of the prodigal son, why didn't the father force his son to come home? Was it perhaps because he didn't love him?

And it came to pass . . .

The message of Christmas

For a Christian, the message heard by the shepherds on the first Christmas was the most important message ever heard in the history of mankind.

> And the angel said to them, 'Be not afraid; for behold, I bring you good news of a great joy which will come to all the people; for to you is born this day in the city of David a Saviour, who is Christ the Lord. And this will be a sign for you: you will find a babe wrapped in swaddling cloths and lying in a manger.   Luke 2: 10–12

What this message will tell us is that the God who created the universe and gave to it order and harmony was now going to 'do something' to recreate order and harmony among men. It is the will of God that we be liberated from our sins and receive from him peace. The name *Jesus* means 'the Lord is salvation'. This event, in which God becomes man and comes to re-establish a broken relationship between man and God and man and his fellow men, is called *the incarnation*.

The prophet Jeremiah spoke of this in these words:

> But this is the covenant which I will make with the house of Israel after those days, says the Lord: I will put my law within them, and I will write it upon their hearts; and I will be their God, and they shall be my people. And no longer shall each man teach his neighbour and each his brother, saying, Know the Lord, for they shall all know me, from the least of them to the greatest, says the Lord; for I will forgive their iniquity, and I will remember their sin no more.   Jeremiah 31: 33–35 (RSV)

The greatest of all . . .

Let's take a look at what God does when he comes to us in Christ. There are good reasons why he does what he does and comes in the way he comes.

If you and I are to be changed, if we are to experience a liberation from the chaos which cripples us, then a radical change must happen inside us.

In the first place we must get rid of the feeling that everything in life is meaningless. We really can't get excited about living up to our potential, or offering ourselves for others if we believe that life, both ours and our neighbour's, is meaningless. It isn't easy just to pull 'meaning' out of a hat like a magician pulls out rabbits. Nor do we want to 'make up something' so that we can pretend that life is meaningful. We want to experience the fact that life *is* meaningful. One of the most meaningful experiences a person can have comes through his faith in God. But to experience faith in God as something meaningful, the God we have faith in can't be just any god who happens to come along. The God in whom we have faith must be a God who can really mean something to us.

By the word 'God' many people mean a higher power. But belief in a higher power does not really mean much to a person. A power, no matter how high or how almighty, is cold, dead and impersonal. It cannot *love* people. It cannot *will* anything for us. When Christianity speaks of a God who 'does something', who redeems us through Christ, it is speaking of another kind of God than just a higher power. A Christian believes in a God who *wills* things for people. A Christian believes in a God who *loves* us.

We can read in the Old Testament, already many hundreds of years before Christ, that according to the Bible, God is not only a God somewhere out there in the universe who created everything. God is not only a higher power: God is much, much more. He is a God who comes to people in the way *that means most to them*. We know, that there are few things in life that mean more to people than love. Think for a minute of how much love of others towards you (or lack of it) has made you what you are. An excellent description of how people in the Old Testament felt God's love and experienced his active care can be seen in the 23rd Psalm.

The Lord is my shepherd, I shall not want;
he makes me lie down in green pastures.
He leads me beside still waters;
He restores my soul.
He leads me in paths of righteousness
for his name's sake.
Even though I walk through the valley
of the shadow of death,
I fear no evil;
for thou art with me;
thy rod and thy staff,
they comfort me.
Thou preparest a table before me
in the presence of my enemies;
thou anointest my head with oil,
my cup overflows.
Surely goodness and mercy shall follow me
all the days of my life;
and I shall dwell in the house of the Lord for ever.

Psalm 23 (RSV)

Why God loves us no-one can say. We can hardly say that we have earned his love by our good works and deeds. Quite the opposite! God's love, which we have in no way earned, is called *the grace* of God.

For discussion

1. Read Luke 15: 1–7. Why were the Pharisees displeased with Jesus?
2. What do you think Jesus meant by the story of the lost sheep?
3. Many believe that Christianity is for 'good', 'moral' and 'religious' people. What do you think?
4. Jesus broke many religious laws. Was Jesus religious?
5. If Jesus came today where do you think you would find him at work?

... is love

One of the most meaningful experiences you can have is to discover yourself as an individual—something that no other person is or can be. There is no one exactly like you. No one has precisely your way of thinking about things, your way of being troubled or even your way of being a sinner. Christianity becomes meaningful to you not as a citizen of a so-called Christian country, nor as a member of a Christian family, nor even as a part of a Christian church. It becomes meaningful when it becomes meaningful to the person and individual that *you* are.

In the New Testament we see Jesus in constant contact with people. These people are met not only in groups or congregations but as individuals. He seems always to have had time and interest for individual persons. There are many examples of this: Jesus and the centurion, Jesus and Matthew, Jesus and the man with the withered hand, Jesus

and Nicodemus, Jesus and the rich young man, Jesus and the thief on the cross, Jesus and Peter after the resurrection, and many, many others.

Class, race, position, nationality and wealth are of no interest to Jesus. There exists for him only *people*. There are only people who need his help, power, love and his fellowship.

When we read, for example in Mark 12:41–44, about the widow's penny we can see that Jesus is not concerned with *how much* a person gives but *how* a person gives. The rich placed large sums in the offerings but from their abundance. The poor widow gave only one penny—all she owned. Therefore, according to Jesus, she gave most.

Those who were most looked down upon in Jesus' time were the publicans (they helped the Roman imperialists with administration and were therefore considered traitors) and sinners (those who did not keep all the religious laws). When Jesus ate with these people, the Pharisees asked how he could do such a thing. He answered, 'Those who are well have no need of a physician, but those who are sick; I came not to call the righteous but sinners.'

If there is ever to be peace and justice on this earth, it will come not just when we make political or economic changes, but when individuals are changed. It is very popular and easy to blame all the troubles of this earth on politics and economics. But a change will take place when Christ 'does something' with you and me as individuals. A change will take place when *we* change.

But the truth can hurt

If God is to do something with us, and if he is to help us and liberate us through Christ, then the first thing we must be willing to do is to accept and admit that there is something wrong with us. We must admit that we are people who create chaos instead of harmony, destroy instead of create, hate instead of love, never forget instead of forgive, and this is what we mean by the word 'sinner'. We must admit that we need peace. If you are sick then you must admit that you are sick and go to a hospital so that you may be cured. I have heard people say that when they go to church they get depressed. They don't like to hear that they are sinners. But we *are* sinners. Would it be better if the pastor just patted people on the back and lied to them? Would you be willing to go to a doctor who didn't tell the truth to his patients because he didn't want to depress them? Never! If we are to get well then we must be willing to look reality straight in the eye.

Many people have the idea that Jesus was a nice sweet man who went around healing the sick and being generally nice to everyone. But this is not the Jesus we meet in the New Testament. When we read about him we discover that he was often an irritating, disturbing, and even painful teacher. He was like this not because he was mean, but because he was a realist and told the truth. He called a spade a spade. But some people don't want to hear the truth about themselves. It is easier and pleasanter to be unreal. Do you dare, for instance, to ask even your very closest friend to tell you precisely and exactly what he or she thinks of you?

Those whom Jesus upset most were precisely those who thought themselves to be the best and purest—the Scribes and Pharisees. They had a great many rules and laws telling a person what he could or could not do. But Jesus saw that theirs was often not religion at all, but just empty words and forms. Jesus says, among other things, to these people:

Woe to you, scribes and Pharisees, hypocrites! for you are like whitewashed tombs, which outwardly appear beautiful, but within they are full of dead men's bones and all uncleanness. So you also outwardly appear righteous to men, but within you are full of hypocrisy and iniquity.

Matthew 23: 27–28 (RSV)

It isn't strange that the Pharisees and scribes wanted to get rid of Jesus. No-one likes to be shown as a hypocrite. But the way in which the scribes and Pharisees got rid of Jesus shows that Jesus spoke the truth about them. They could not kill him. That was forbidden. But they could fix things so that Jesus would be suspected of revolution by the Roman leaders and then *they* could kill him. In this way they could get rid of Jesus, but still be considered innocent and righteous.

We must not flee from reality and truth about ourselves. To flee is no solution. We must see ourselves and look the stupid things we do straight in the eye without trying to explain away our guilt, or burden someone else with it. *This hurts—but is necessary.* You will never discover God's help and liberation if you won't admit that you need help and liberation.

For discussion

1. What did Jesus mean when he said, 'Those who are well have no need of a physician, but those who are sick; I came not to call the righteous but sinners'?
2. Was the doctor's kindness spoken of on page 51 the same as love? Explain your answer?
3. People sometimes say, 'I don't like to go to church and hear about sin. Why can't ministers talk about something happier?' What would you reply to such a person?
4. Read John 3: 16–21. Why was Jesus hated by many?

'I conquered only land, Jesus conquered the hearts of men'

If you take a close look at people you will discover that they are strange creatures. On the one hand they are geniuses who can solve the most impossible problems with the aid of technology and science. On the other hand they are 'moral idiots'.

Think about it!

Man is so smart that he can split the atom—at the same time he is so stupid that he can build atomic bombs and *use them*.
Man is so brilliant that he can land on the moon—at the same time he can't live in peace with his own family.

We would like to believe that man gets better as soon as he receives education, more information, more reason. But it's not that easy. We can hardly say that we, who place men on the moon, do heart transplants, and split the atom, lack brains, education or reason. What is missing is control over the reason, education and brains man already has. The problem lies in the will of man, in his heart. The famous scientist, Albert Einstein, once wrote: 'The problem is not the atomic bomb. The problem is the heart of man.'

Jesus put it this way;

For no good tree bears bad fruit, nor again does a bad tree bear good fruit; for each tree is known by its own fruit. For figs are not gathered from thorns, nor are grapes picked from a bramble bush. The good man out of the good treasure of his heart produces good, and the evil man out of his evil treasure produces evil; for out of the abundance of the heart his mouth speaks.

Luke 6: 43–45 (RSV)

This is why, when God acts, he does something that is meant to reach the heart of man. He wants to reach us on the level of our feelings and wills. He wants to reach our hate, our pride, our fear, and egoism, where strife is born. To reach us in our hearts and to reach us deeply God chooses *love*. We know from our own experience that nothing reaches us so deeply and with such transforming power as *love*. Nothing characterizes Jesus more than his love, especially when he suffers and dies for us on the cross.

We meet Jesus' love everywhere in the New Testament. For example, when he says:

'You have heard that it was said, You shall love your neighbour and hate your enemy. But I say to you, Love your enemies and pray for those who persecute you, so that you may be sons of your Father who is in heaven; for he makes his sun rise on the evil and on the good, and sends rain on the just and the unjust.'

Matthew 5: 43–44 (RSV)

We see the love of Christ in his parables of the Prodigal Son and the Good Samaritan.

We see his love in his deeds. We see it in how he heals the sick, the blind and the lame and how he receives the adulterous woman with forgiveness.

But the most moving event of all, the one that speaks to our very depths, is Christ's suffering and death on the cross. The drama and love of the cross reaches people everywhere on earth and in all periods of history in a way that words or mere teaching or preaching never can. The cross speaks to us of man's stupidity which destroys the very best and highest that man has. It speaks to us of God's love, which in spite of injustice, dirt, evil, hate and pain, can still say as Christ said on the cross: 'Father forgive them; for they know not what they do.'

What Jesus taught was not all that new. He quotes and uses much of the Old Testament. It is what he *is* and what he *does* and *the way he does it* that is new. This is also the message of Christianity, our gospel or good news.

You may feel that the cross was for Christ a defeat, a symbol of his failure. But this is not so. It is quite the opposite! The cross was Jesus' victory. Napoleon put it this way: 'I conquered only land, Jesus conquered the hearts of men.'

We do not celebrate the death of Napoleon nor of Alexander the

Great nor of the famous philosopher Socrates. But each year, all over the earth, people celebrate Good Friday—Jesus' victory on the cross.

For discussion

1. 'It's not *what* you know but *who* you know that is important'. But Jesus—who did he make friends with? Was this foolish?
2. Many say: 'If you want to change the world you must use force—seize power.' But Jesus—how does he arrive at Jerusalem (see Luke 19: 29–38)? Was it foolish of Jesus not to have an army with him?
3. Instead of becoming king Jesus let himself be executed. Was this foolish?
4. Millions of people have been executed throughout history. Why is a 'foolish' man like Jesus remembered?

Crucifix carved in wood
at the art school in Cyrene
Rhodesia.

But it is so hard to understand . . .

It is not easy to understand why Jesus should die on the cross. Why should he suffer and die for me? The cross seems so grim and meaningless.

But one thing is sure. The drama of the cross speaks to us in a way that really goes in. It speaks not just to our heads but to our hearts and feelings.

A story that shows how suffering speaks to us tells of a mother and her eight-year-old daughter. The mother was trying to help her daughter with something but the girl just got angry. She refused to stay in the room and listen. She went angrily upstairs to her room. On the way to her room she saw on her mother's bed a new expensive dress that her mother was going to wear the same evening. Nearby lay a pair of scissors her mother had been using. The girl took the scissors and cut the dress into small pieces. After a while the girl's mother came upstairs and discovered what she had done. She was of course deeply hurt and sad. She laid down on the bed and wept. This was *not* the reaction the daughter had expected. Soon she went quietly and slowly into her mother's room and whispered anxiously 'Mother'. Her mother didn't answer but just continued to cry. She said again, 'Mother, Mother'. After a few seconds her mother answered, 'What do you want?' 'Take me back, mother, please take me back,' the girl pleaded.

Sorrow and tears had spoken to the girl in a very special way. Do you believe that the daughter would have experienced the same feelings if her mother had been furious and struck her? Do you think she would have felt the same if her mother had said, 'Now I am going to teach you some rules on how to behave? For example,

1. You must not play with the scissors. You can cut yourself.
2. You must not cut new dresses into pieces. They cost losts of money.

3. You must not spread cut pieces of material around on the floor because it looks messy.

Jesus did not come to judge and punish people. Neither did he come just to give us some new words of wisdom. He came to suffer a painful and unjust death on the cross so that he could show us the end-result of our deeds and in this way reach us. He wanted to reach us with, among other things, his words on the Cross:

'Father forgive them for they know not what they do.'

This is the same suffering, sacrificing Christ we receive at communion. When you take communion you are met there not with threats of punishments and hell nor with words of wisdom. The pastor says:

'The body of Christ offered for you'
'The blood of Christ shed for your sins.'

Paul says of the Cross in the first letter to the Corinthians:

'For the word of the cross is folly to those who are perishing, but to us who are being saved it is the power of God. . . .
For the foolishness of God is wiser than men, and the weakness of God is stronger than men.'

For discussion

1. How would the girl who cut up her mother's dress have been changed if her mother had said to her: 'I am very sorry about this. I am going to give you a present if you promise never to do such a thing again'?
2. 'For the foolishness of God is wiser than men, and the weakness of God is stronger than men.' What does this mean?
3. Was the cross a defeat or a victory for Jesus? What do you think?

The power and mystery of Jesus

It is not always possible to explain everything about Jesus and what God does through him. There are many things that just can't be explained. We believe without demanding complete explanations—just as one falls in love without demanding explanations or scientific evidence. In religion we call things which we believe but cannot understand, a *mystery* or mysterium.

We have a deep need to experience mystery—something higher and beyond our ability to understand or explain. Much of our lives and the world around is a mystery: they cannot be fully explained. Much of what Jesus did is not easy to explain either.

How could Jesus perform miracles? How could he heal the sick, the blind and the lame? How could he transform two fishes and five loaves of bread into food for 5,000? How could he raise Lazarus from the dead? How could he himself rise from the dead? These things seem unbelievable and impossible. And if Jesus was only an ordinary person like you and me and was in no way the God who created the universe then these things *were* impossible for him. But if what the New Testament says is true, if Jesus is (as the church expresses it) the Son of God, are these miracles—even a resurrection from the dead—impossible? Hardly! Can we really say that a resurrection *is impossible* for the God who created the universe, and even life itself? *Hardly*! You and I can't do this kind of miracle. But then we cannot even create one single seed either, can we?

Actually, Jesus' power to perform miracles is much easier to believe in than his power to forgive us our sins and give us peace, almost 2,000 years after he walked this earth.

There are few greater needs today than the need of peace and forgiveness. We cannot begin to serve or love our neighbour and rise to our potential if we have not ourselves experienced an inner peace. You know, yourself, how nervous you become when the people you are with are nervous and unsettled. The opposite is also true. We have a much easier time finding peace if the people around us radiate this peace. Guilt feelings hinder this experience. We feel we must always defend ourselves, and therefore always present a false front. We have created chaos instead of harmony, hate and division instead of love. We long for forgiveness—not only from other people but from God.

Jesus was not just a man who lived 2,000 years ago. He lives! He arose from the dead on Easter day. This means that his love and forgiveness are just as living and healing today as they were 2,000 years ago.

It was precisely this power in Jesus to forgive that shocked the scribes and the Pharisees. How could a *man* do such a thing? How can even Jesus' sacrifice on the cross mean forgiveness and atonement for our sins? We don't really know how this works in practice, but it is Christianity's greatest and most important miracle. The only thing I can say is that in some strange way many people have found that it works. It has worked for almost 2,000 years and works today in the same living and powerful way. If it were not for this living forgiveness that people experience through Christ, he would have been forgotten a long time ago. This is 'The peace of God which passeth all understanding'.

Paul writes of this power:

> For I am sure that neither death, nor life, nor angels, nor principalities, nor things present, nor things to come, nor powers, nor height, nor depth, nor anything else in all creation, will be able to separate us from the love of God in Christ Jesus our Lord.
>
> Romans 8: 38–39 (RSV)

For discussion

1. Read John 20: 19–29. How did the disciples feel?
2. What changed Thomas?
3. Read Matthew 28: 11–15. How did the Jews explain Jesus' resurrection?
4. The disciples could of course have done this and fooled everyone. But do you think they could, by doing this, fool themselves and find inspiration to become preachers of a risen Christ? Or did their inspiration come from their experience of what Jesus promises in verse 20? What do you think?

Did God succeed?

When we ask, 'Did God succeed in doing something to liberate us?' we must remember what it is that God is trying to do. The disciples did not understand this. Most people don't understand it today either. The disciples didn't understand what kind of Messiah Jesus was supposed to be. Some thought that he was supposed to become a king or a great leader, perhaps a general, to help the Jews in their liberation from the Romans. Others assumed (and still assume) that his main and most important task was to be a great teacher. But his task and goal were much higher and greater than people dreamed. He was to create a kingdom—the kingdom of God. It was not going to be for one particular race or people, nor was it to be any particular political kingdom. The kingdom of God was to include all peoples and all races. It was to reach over all borders and political differences. This kingdom was to be *within* people—in their hearts. When the Pharisees asked Jesus when the kingdom of God was to come he answered:

> The kingdom of God does not come in such a way as to be seen. No one will say, Look, here it is! or, here it is!; because the Kingdom of God is within you.
>
> Luke 17: 20–21—(Good News for Modern Man)

Whether God's attempt to do something succeeds or not, depends on whether this attempt reaches you in your heart, your will and your feelings. When this happens people are converted. When Jesus said to Nicodemus that a person must be born again to see the kingdom of God, and when Paul called Christians 'new creatures', they meant *exactly* what they said. Do you remember in the beginning of this book about the young people who saw incorrectly because they hated? (The knife that 'jumped' from the white man's hand to the black man's hand). This example tells us that our feelings determine not only what we think and feel but also even what our eyes see and our ears hear.

To be converted, or to become a new creature, means to *see* and *hear* in a new way. This is the way God succeeds in changing people. It does not happen by reading *about* Jesus or even learning by heart what he said. It happens when we become partakers in a new relationship with him. It happens through our experience of his love, forgiveness and presence in our lives. Do you dare become a part of this kingdom o. God? Do you dare allow him to make drastic changes in you and your life?

It is of this kind of recreated people that Aristides of Athens wro in or about A.D. 137.

> They know God and trust in God. They conciliate their oppresso and win them over to friends. They do good to their enemie Their wives live pure lives and their daughters are modest. Th men do not participate in impurity or unlawful practices. The persuade their servants and their servants' children to becom Christians through the love their faith gives them. Converte servants are without exception called 'brothers and sisters'. The do not refuse to help widows. They rescue orphans so that the

are not exploited. They gladly help all who are in need. Yes, they even starve and go without in order to help others. Towards strangers they practise a wonderful hospitality and they do this with joy. They look upon all men as brothers in spirit and in God. They obey carefully the commandments of their Messiah. . . . Their good deeds are not done to show off. They seek, to the contrary, to keep their deeds of love from being publicly noticed. This is indeed a new people in which something divine lives.

Much that is a result of God's 'success' is taken for granted by us today. We don't give a second thought to the fact that we have hospitals and that we care for the sick. But these things have not always existed. Care for the sick is founded on an idea that has not always existed, nor existed everywhere on earth. It is founded on an idea of the value of human life and of our responsibility to our neighbour, no matter who that neighbour might be. It is the idea we found so clearly in the parable of the Good Samaritan. People have always looked after themselves, their own family or tribe or clan. This parable says to us that *anyone* in need of help is our neighbour, but this idea first began to work only when there were people who had been changed — people with whom God had succeeded in doing something. These people saw things differently and *acted* differently than had been the case before.

A good deal of the democracy we take for granted is built upon a Christian ideal. It is built, for example, on what Paul says in Galatians 3:28:

There is neither Jew nor Greek, there is neither slave nor free, there is neither male nor female; for you are all one in Christ Jesus.

Greece had a highly developed culture long before Christ was born, but the democracy of the Greeks was for only 30,000 of the 400,000 who lived in Athens. And they didn't think there was anything wrong in leaving unwanted children out in the woods to die.

For discussion

1. Jesus's *mission* was not to become a king, not even to be a great teacher. *I am Jesus mission*! What does this mean?
2. Where is God's kingdom?
3. Did God succeed?

But why have there been wars between Christians?

This is a very common question. It cannot be denied that a large part of the history of the church is a scandal. War, murder, prisons and even torture have been both supported and blessed by the church. These awful things have happened when the leaders of the church have forgotten that the kingdom of God is within people, and that power and violence cannot *force* people to this inner change.

Someone cries out, 'Here, under this flag and creed, is the kingdom of God!'

Someone else says, 'No! Here it is under this king and according to these dogmas and teachings!'

Christianity has often been something that different power groups, countries, and church leaders have used for their own selfish purposes. When Christianity *itself* is transformed, so that it ceases to be a power for transformation, it becomes worthless. That war and much evil have come from the churches and have received their blessing, does not mean that Christianity is false. It means that it has not been practised. It is the experience of the church that man is a sinner and that he tries the best he can to destroy, exploit, and corrupt almost everything. The crucifixion of Christ speaks to us of this.

But we should never try to sweep the scandals of the church under the carpet. These scandals must be in clear view to remind us contantly how easy Christianity, as well as much else that is good, can be changed into something quite different.

When Christianity really works, radical changes take place. Christianity has succeeded in inspiring people to sacrifice themselves for others. An example of this sacrificing is the missionary work of the church.

It has recently become very 'in' to take an interest in the under-developed countries. But the church has been active in missionary work in these countries for a very long time. There are many who are *interested* in helping these countries and peoples. But how many are willing to sacrifice their security, status symbols, and comforts in order actually to *do something*. For the most part, those who have done something have been Christians.

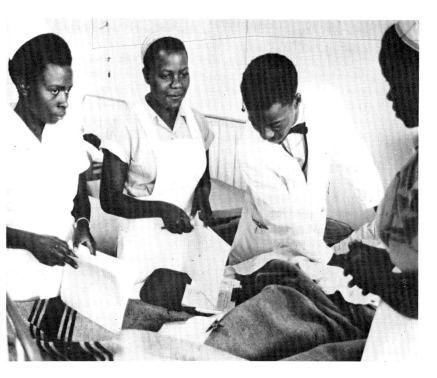

Is there anything in history that can be compared to the missions of the church? People have always gone to other countries to *take*—power, land, wealth, and peoples—but it is only within the missions of the church that people have gone to other countries to *give* and *help*. They have built hospitals, schools, and churches. They have healed people and taught them how to read. Missionaries have offered their lives for these people who are also *our* neighbours. Would you be willing to do this? It is one thing to give money to the poor in the underdeveloped countries, or to feel sorry for them. But to offer your life for these people is something else. To do this demands a miracle—a miracle in the hearts and wills of men.

Whether God's transforming miracle succeeds or not depends on whether we allow it to happen within us. What about you?

For discussion

1. What is the difference between foreign aid and mission work?
2. 'I can understand the church building hospitals and schools in poor countries but why waste the money on building churches?' How would you answer this?

But how can we know that all this is true?

No doubt, all this about God's forgiveness, peace, transforming fellowship, and power over death, sounds great. But how can we know if all this is true? What proof is there that what I have told you so far is true? There is no proof in the ordinary meaning of the word. I can *prove* nothing. Does that mean that it is false? No, not at all. It means simply that faith is one of those things that we don't prove to one another, but each one himself must experience it as something that is true. Demanding proof for everything in order for it to be important or true is like saying to someone: 'You must choose; either you are to become a scientist or you may fall in love.'

Let me put it this way. If I could *prove* to you that God exists, that Jesus was God's attempt to do something, and that salvation and the peace of God were real and true, then I would stop being a pastor. Perhaps that sounds strange. 'Isn't it the pastor's job to try to prove all this for people?', I can hear you ask. No, because then you wouldn't have to get really involved and commit yourself.

A pastor can show you the way to go, tell you about God's love and peace. He can tell you what he himself has experienced, but he may not and cannot prove anything to you. You wouldn't hire someone to fall in love for you and then try and tell you about love and prove to you that love exists. *You* want to fall in love. *You* want to experience love. This is your personal right. You have also a personal right to experience faith yourself as something real, living, and transforming. Neither the pastor nor anyone else can do this for you.

As we said in the introduction, you don't want to marry someone just because some computer decides that this would be right. You want your feelings to be involved also. You want to fall in love. Those things which reach us deepest are things like love and faith. They reach into both our feelings and our personalities.

For discussion

1. Someone says to you: 'Prove Christianity and I will believe it.' How would you answer this statement?
2. How are love and faith alike?

On the edge of the Grand Canyon

Faith is to take a step without proof

Many people have a wrong idea about what Christianity means by *faith* or *belief* in God. They ask: 'Do you believe in God?' But what they mean is, 'Are you of the opinion that a God exists?' If you do, they consider you a 'believer'. But this is wrong. An *opinion* that God exists is not worth much. To believe in God, according to Christianity, means faith, trust and commitment. It is a whole way of life, not just an opinion. A cowboy in Arizona once described faith to a pastor like this:

> Faith is like standing on the edge of the Grand Canyon. It drops off 1,500 feet right before you. While you are admiring the view, the low shrub forest behind you catches on fire. The wind is blowing towards you and the fire has you surrounded and is moving your way. There is no escape. The smoke from the fire begins to fill the canyon in front of you and you can no longer see the bottom. You don't know what to do. Suddenly you hear a voice from down in the canyon that says 'Jump! I'll catch you.' You look carefully over the edge but you can see nothing through the smoke. Once again you hear the voice. 'Just step over the edge! I'll take care of you.'

To take a step without proof—without seeing, trusting the one who calls—this is Christian faith.

I would gladly push you over the edge. But that wouldn't be the same thing, would it? You must take this step yourself. The only thing I can do is to lead you to the edge and tell you what I experienced when I took the step, but I cannot *prove* that what I say is true. You can experience what faith is only when *you* take this step. It is only then that God can reveal himself and his help. We don't create faith ourselves. It is God's presence that makes faith living. It is the Holy Spirit. But by taking this step of trust and faith we make ourselves receptive to God's love and presence. Luther begins his explanation of the third Article of the Creed like this:

> I believe that I cannot by my own reason or strength believe in Jesus Christ, my Lord, or come to Him; but the Holy Spirit has called me through the Gospel, enlightened me with His gifts, and sanctified and preserved me in the true faith. . . .

Don't get the idea that this *step of faith* happens once and then it is over once and for all. Faith is a relationship. It must 'happen' daily. It is like love. There is often a single moment when you can say: 'It was then that I fell in love.' But no-one in his right mind would say: 'Well that's that, now it is finished.' To fall in love and marry someone is for life. Each day demands sacrifice, trust, love, and understanding. This is the way of faith as well. You will doubt, and think at times that the whole thing is mad and much too demanding. But faith in God takes in all your life and your whole personality. A belief that does not take in the whole person and his life is called hypocrisy.

Faith is Love

I don't know how it came about that for so many people belief in God has come to mean an opinion that God exists. It certainly doesn't say this in the Bible: Jesus never said it. And the church has never interpreted *belief* or *faith* as if it were only an opinion. Christian faith or belief means a deep sense of faith and trust. It also means love. To 'know the Lord' is an expression used throughout the Old Testament. It means that we should have a relationship with God and not just believe that he exists.

The Bible also says: 'You shall *love* the Lord your God with all your heart, and with all your soul, and with all your strength, and with all your mind; and your neighbour as yourself.' It does not say we should be of strong opinions. After the resurrection Jesus did *not* ask Peter, 'Do you believe that I am arisen?' nor, 'Are you now of the opinion that God has power over death?' Jesus asks Peter three times: 'Do you *love* me?' Someone has written: 'He who does not know God has loved him too little.' Christian faith is a relationship or fellowship with God.

70

What would you say if you met a friend who told you that he and a girl whom you also knew were in love with another and yet you had never seen them together. You would ask him: 'Have you been out with her a lot lately?' He answers: 'No I never have.' 'But', you ask surprised, 'you surely write or ring one another up often?' 'No, never,' is his answer, 'But I believe she exists!' To believe in God means not just to believe that God exists but that you and your life have something to do with him. You trust him, speak to him when you pray, seek to do his will and live in fellowship with him.

Faith is the work of the Holy Spirit

There are many who say that faith is only an illusion or wishful thinking. But they are speaking of something they themselves have never experienced. They sound a bit like a seven-year-old child who teases his teenage brother because he has a girl friend. Little brother thinks girls and love are stupid, but just wait a few years and he will change his tune. Faith, as with love, must be experienced to be understood.

How does faith happen? Do people see a bright light like Paul? No, not often. Generally we grow into faith slowly and over a long period of time. Sometimes it happens all at once, like love at first sight.

The important thing is not to give up and be apathetic but as Paul says,

> Keep on working, with fear and trembling, to complete your salvation, For God is always at work in you to make you willing and able to obey his own purpose.
>
> Philippians 2: 12–13 (Good News for Modern Man)

Many come to faith by reading the Bible, some through church services, others through partaking of communion. Some become believers alone, perhaps out in the countryside somewhere. Faith is very individual. Many can say *when* it happened, others only *that* it happened.

It is through faith that we discover God's action in our lives and understand what Jesus meant when he said,

> If you love me, you will obey my commandments. I will ask the Father, and he will give you another Helper, the Spirit of truth, to stay with you forever. The world cannot receive him, because it

cannot see him or know him. But you know him, for he remains with you and lives in you. I will not leave you alone; I will come back to you. In a little while the world will see me no more, but you will see me; and because I live, you also will live. When that day comes, you will know that I am in my Father, and that you are in me, just as I am in you.

John 14: 15–20 (Good News for Modern Man)

Faith gives us a deep feeling of peace and harmony, but at the same time a responsibility and desire to tell the good news to somebody else. We experience what Jesus meant when he said,

Come to me, all of you who are tired from carrying your heavy loads, and I will give you rest. Take my yoke and put it on you, and learn from me, for I am gentle and humble in spirit; and you will find rest. The yoke I will give you is easy and the load I will put on you is light.

Matthew 11: 28 (Good News for Modern Man)

Is there anything more important for people to experience today than this, the third article of the creed?

I believe in the Holy Ghost; the Holy Catholic Church, the communion of saints; the forgiveness of sins; the resurrection of the body; and the life everlasting.

For discussion

1. What is the difference between what Christianity means by the word 'believe' and what we mean when we say 'I believe it will rain today.'?
2. The week before you are to get married your fiancé says to you, 'Look, I'm willing to marry you but first I would like you to go to a doctor and take a blood test to see if you have the right hormones in your blood and prove to me that you are in love with me.' What would you answer? Explain your answer.

'Consider the birds'

God's guidance and will

Think how many people worry about tomorrow. We know nothing for sure about what the future will bring. Although we might not find it so hard to believe in God and the power of God, we still find it difficult to believe Jesus when he says,

> Therefore I tell you, do not be anxious about your life, what you shall eat or what you shall drink, nor about your body, what you shall put on. Is not life more than food, and the body more than clothing? Look at the birds of the air; they neither sow nor reap nor gather into barns, and yet your heavenly Father feeds them. Are you not of more value than they?   Matthew 6: 25 (RSV)

We want guarantees and security for the future. But in the Lord's Prayer Jesus says that we should pray 'Thy will be done', and 'Give us this day our *daily* bread'. This is to believe in the guidance of God.

Many people don't like this idea about God's guidance and care. If God exists, they ask why it is that he allows sickness and poverty?

But people who say this seem to imply that all rich and all healthy people are happy and have peace. Is this true? Are health and wealth the key to happiness? Of course not. Money and health can be just as harmful to people as poverty and sickness. It all depends on *how* we are rich and *how* we are poor, *how* we are healthy and *how* we are sick. A person can be poor or sick and from this become bitter and full of hate. A person can be rich and healthy and from this become proud and blind to others who need help.

Some journalists once interviewed Milton Eisenhower, President Eisenhower's brother. They asked him about what kind of childhood the Eisenhowers had experienced. One journalist asked: 'Is it true, that you were poor when you were children?' The answer was, 'Oh no! We weren't poor. We just didn't have any money.'

There are few things in life that are in themselves either good or bad. So much depends on *how* we react to those things that life throws at us. I have read of people who even experienced Hitler's concentration camps as something positive and meaningful. It was for them an occasion really to serve their fellow prisoners.

God guides us in three ways. First, by changing the ways in which we react to what happens to us. We may react like the devil or we may react like God. One way creates chaos, the other way creates harmony.

If sickness strikes we can think like this: 'What lousy luck' God knows how long I'll have to lie here. Not only is it a drag, but look at the money I am losing.' Such a person is filled with bitterness and anxiety. But we could react like this: 'This is sure costing me something, I know that. But I've some time now to rest and think. There aren't many who have time for that nowadays. Maybe I'll meet some interesting people here, too. Maybe there is someone here whom I could help. I know there are lots of people who are lonely'.

Secondly, God guides us by leading us on the right paths. God has a goal for us. He guides us, through the people we meet, what we hear on the radio, or see on TV, through books we read, and in many, many ways.

Third, God leads us by occasionally coming into our lives with his presence and power. This is what happened when Paul was converted. This happens when we experience the living Christ.

What is God's will for you? Where will he lead you? Will you give him freedom to be active in your life?

> I don't know Who or What put the question, I don't know when it was put. I don't even remember answering. But at some moment I did answer *Yes* to Someone or Something and from that hour I was certain that existence is meaningful and that, therefore, my life, in self surrender, had a goal.
>
> From that moment I have known what it means not to look back, and to take no thought for the morrow.
>
> Dag Hammarskjöld, Whitsunday, 1961

For discussion

1. What did Eisenhower's brother mean with his answer?
2. What did Hammarskjöld mean when he spoke of 'not to look back' and 'to take no thought for the morrow.'?
3. How can this experience give a person peace?

'I prayed for all things, that I might enjoy life'

I asked God for strength, that I might achieve,
I was made weak, that I might learn humbly to obey . . .
I asked for health, that I might do greater things,
I was given infirmity, that I might do better things . . .
I asked for riches, that I might be happy.
I was given poverty, that I might be wise . . .
I asked for power, that I might have the praise of men,
I was given weakness, that I might feel the need of God . . .
I asked for all things, that I might enjoy life,
I was given life, that I might enjoy all things . . .
I got nothing that I asked for, but everything I had hoped for.
Almost despite myself, my unspoken prayers were answered.
I am among all men, most richly blessed.

An unknown soldier in the American Civil War

Some people think that it is childish to pray to God. In a way they are right: Jesus says that we must be as children.

A person is really grown up when he is no longer afraid of being child-like. He doesn't have to act tough any more to convince others and above all, himself, that he is grown up. He can, like a child, admit that he needs help, that he is afraid, alone, and mean. It isn't so hard to pray. You don't even have to fold your hands, although it helps sometimes. You don't have to be in church or know any special religious words. All you have to do is tell God about you and your life in your own words. If you still find it difficult to pray, use a prayer that is written, one that perhaps many others have used. The prayer used most in Christianity is, of course, the one Jesus taught his disciples.

Our Father

Our Father, who art in heaven, hallowed by Thy name; Thy kingdom come; Thy will be done on earth as it is in heaven; give us this day our daily bread; and forgive us our trespasses as we forgive those who trespass against us; and lead us not into temptation; but deliver us from evil; for Thine is the kingdom, and the power, and the glory, for ever and ever. Amen.

Table grace at the
Martin Luther King
home.

Three different ways

The Trinity

We have spoken of three different ways of experiencing God. We spoke first of God the Creator or Father who has created a universe of order and harmony. Much of this we cannot fathom or understand.

We have also spoken of a God of love who through Jesus Christ attempts to 'do something'. Here we see a God who is not just a distant higher power, but a God who reaches out to us with his love. The church has always used the expression, 'God's Son', for Jesus Christ.

We have also spoken of experiencing God, not only as a creating power somewhere in space, or as Jesus Christ who died and rose 2,000 years ago, but also a God *who is active today* through the Holy Spirit.

We experience God in three different ways. This is what the church means when it teaches that God is triune—a trinity—three but still one. A triangle is often seen in churches as a symbol for the trinity.

For discussion

1. Read carefully, 'I asked God for strength' and the Lord's Prayer. Name three things we *should not* pray for and three things we *should* pray for.
2. Write your own prayer using the answer to question 1.

The Bible was written by many

The Bible is the word of God

What shape is the earth? Is it round! Everyone knows that the earth is round. Now look up Isaiah 11: 12 and Revelation 7: 1 in your Bible. Here you read that the earth has corners—four corners! We know that a ball (which is round) doesn't have any corners. How can the earth be round if the Bible says that it has four corners? Shall we throw out everything our scientists have told us about the shape of the earth? Or shall we throw out our Bibles? Actually we don't have to throw out anything, except perhaps some misunderstandings on our part. The first thing we must get straight is that the Bible is not a book of science. It is neither a textbook in biology, nor in geology. Those who wrote the Bible were not scientists. Their interest was man's relationship to God and to one another. The second thing we must remember is that those who wrote the Bible used various expressions just as we do today. Perhaps you have said sometime, 'These biscuits are hard as rocks'. Did you mean that they *really* were as hard as granite? No! You meant that they were inedible, but not that they actually were as hard as rocks.

Remember that the Bible is a collection of books written by many different authors, using different ways of expressing themselves. The Bible is not an easy book to understand, but we don't have to make it more difficult than it is. Sometimes the Bible is written like a newspaper, sometimes like a poem, and sometimes like a saga. Let's take a modern example of how the same experience can be formed or written in three different ways. We can take the same event and see how three people, a journalist, an author, and a poet use different forms to tell of or describe the same thing. First the journalist:

A great fire raged through the Northeast residential area of Centerville today, taking hundreds of lives and destroying millions of dollars' worth of property. A strong north wind hampered the efforts of the fire fighters to bring the flames under control. Tonight, hundreds of Red Cross workers converged on the charred city to bring aid to the stricken victims.

This is the kind of factual description we meet in the Bible when we read Luke 2: 1–7. This is written as history.

An author might describe the same event like this:

The loud flames bid the winds welcome, while trees mourned and hills grimaced in pain. A remnant of the living tried valiantly to silence the mouths of the flames but fell useless under the belching breath of the conqueror. While midst the chaos stood a band of angels, binding up the wounds of the fallen.

This is the kind of description we find in Isaiah 55: 12.

A poet might write something like this of this same event:

O torturous memory of searing flames
and the cries of the dying;
Be gone and let us rest;
What bleakness thou hast cast upon us,
And cruel wind, why dids't thou visit us
in this ill-appointed hour?
Why didst thou choose to heap sorrow
upon sorrow?
But for the angels of mercy crossed in red,
We might all have gone down in pits.
O torturous memory of searing flames
and the cries of the dying,
Begone and let us rest.*

This is similar to the way Judges 5: 15–18 is written.

Is any one of the above forms of description *truer* than the others? Do you think the author who wrote of 'trees mourning' was trying to fool people? Was he just 'having us on'?

The answer to both of these questions is 'no'. They all want to tell us something truthfully. They just choose to express themselves in different ways.

* With permission of Bethel Bible Series Madison Wisconsin.

80

The important thing to remember is that the Bible was written by many different people, at different times and in different forms. The story of creation, for example, is a form which makes use of an ancient story, not to lead people astray, but to express the truth that God created everything, and that we humans are sinners. The creation story is not biology, geology, nor is it even history. It is a song of praise.

When we say, 'The Bible is the word of God,' we don't mean that God said to Moses, 'Moses: Write down now what I tell you!' We mean that it is God's word, in that it deals with how people in the Bible meet God, experience his power, will, love, and peace. We meet God's word through the people in the Bible and their experiences of God. The Bible tells us about the Jews as God's people, about the disciples and the first Christians, about a missionary called Paul. These are not just ordinary events. They deal with God's activity in and through people. It is God's word because what it says is true about men and about God. It is just as true today as it was 2,000 years ago.

Although we live in a so-called modern age with an advanced technology, man has not really changed very much. Like Adam, we still want *our* wills to dominate. Like David, some men are interested in other men's wives. Like the Pharisees, we are dishonest with ourselves. Like Paul, we are temperamental. We are still like Isaiah, who stood in awe before creation; like the shepherds, who with joy and curiosity came to the crib: like the thieves on the cross, one bitter and evil, the other humble and repentant. And God's grace and love are just as real and living today as always.

You must come to God's word as you come before a mirror. You need to see yourself there. You must come to the word with *expectation* of God's presence and forgiveness. Then you will discover that the Bible is not just another book, but is in fact the word of God.

For discussion

1. If it could be proved that the Good Samaritan or the Prodigal Son never really existed but that Jesus made up these stories, could we then say that they were untrue and worthless? Explain your answer.
2. In what way is the Bible true?
3. What is meant when the Bible is called 'the word of God'?

England begins in San Francisco with BOAC

On life after death

Sometimes people ask the pastor: 'How can you really know anything about heaven or about life after death? You have never been there.' This is, of course, true. We pastors *have* never been there. It is also very confusing for people when they think of heaven, with streets of gold, people with wings, and all kinds of strange things.

Is it really possible for a person to *know* something about life after death—heaven and hell? In a way we can *know* something about it even though we haven't been there. Let me show you what I mean.

Several years ago, when I was in California, I saw a big advertisement in a newspaper in San Francisco. Across the page in bold letters were the words, 'England begins in San Francisco with BOAC.' What did they mean? They meant that when flying from San Francisco to England on BOAC, you fly with others who have the same destination. The plane's crew are English, the food is English, the dishes and the language spoken are English. Even if you have never been in England, you will learn something about England on the way there.

It is the same with heaven. We can learn something about heaven before we get there, since we are on our way there in God's kingdom. We experience his forgiveness and love, his power to create order, his care and guidance. We are on our way there with other Christians who experience the same things. We can know something about heaven, not because we have been there, but because we experience God's presence *here and now.*

The same thing can be said of hell. If hell is, as many say, to be separated from God's harmony and love, then there are many who now experience a kind of hell.

For discussion

1. If some day in the future you were to discover a medicine to stop people from getting old and dying, what would you do with your discovery?
2. *When* is heaven and *when* is hell?

Christianity as revolution

When Christianity has really worked, it has been one of the most revolutionary powers on earth. We live in an era which is in dire need of this revolution. And we live in an unbelievably dangerous time. There are so many atomic bombs today, that all the people on earth could be wiped out many times over if they were to be used. We live in an unjust world. Some areas of the world live in tremendous wealth and well-being, and other areas live in poverty, sickness and constant want. There are no logical reasons why the world should be like this. It is a result of feelings such as greed, fear, pride, suspicion, and hate. What is needed is a revolution that reaches these feelings. The answer lies not only on the political or economic level, but also in the hearts of men. It makes no difference if it is a yellow, black, or white hand that paints the word 'HATE': It remains as 'hate.' Hatred may be painted in red, or blue or any other political colour, but it is still hatred. It is this hatred that the Christian revolution wants to reach. This revolution in our hearts and wills *must* take place if we are ever to live in a world of peace and well-being.

What the Christian revolution can mean for you and your neighbour

It is not just for the sake of the world at large that we must experience a change. There are other reasons much nearer home. This revolution relates to daily contact.

First, no-one lives on an island. We are each day in contact with one another. This contact either helps or hurts those we meet. It is a contact which creates either peace and harmony or unrest, tension, and chaos. Some people don't believe in this: They say that they are *free*! They say, 'I am free—I can do whatever I like.' But to think like this is not far from a kind of thinking that would say, 'I'll run down anyone I want to. It's my car!'

You are not free. You do not live isolated from others. You have a responsibility not only to yourself but to the people with whom you come into contact. You even have a responsibility to those who may need your help, but with whom you are *not* in contact. You must seek those who need you and your help.

Secondly, you need your neighbour. No-one can bear the burden of being alone. Our greatest need is to be loved. We need one another in order to show one another reality and truth. You use your neighbour daily as a kind of mirror. You lay out before him your opinions, feelings, and fears, and he lays out his and you both compare. It is in this way that we begin to understand ourselves. We need this know-ledge. We need to know ourselves. Strange as it may seem, we often know more about others than we know about ourselves. Think how it feels when you hear someone talking about you, and you know that they don't realize that you are present. How you strain your ears to hear everything they say! Why? If you were sure of yourself, and really knew who you were, you wouldn't have such a strong desire to listen. But you *are* unsure of how you appear in the eyes and thoughts of others, and that's why you listen. People who are very isolated often develop two characteristics—unreality and bitterness.

Thirdly, you need to love in order to feel that you are somehow living up to your potential as a human being. There are few things in life that give so much meaning as doing something, *not* just for selfish purposes or because it feels good, but simply because the thing is *right* and *good* in itself. People who don't live for others often feel that life is meaningless and empty. A modern tragedy is the person who says, 'I am free: I'll do what I want to', but who then discovers that he doesn't *want to do anything*.

Fourthly, the Christian faith is not just some lovely idea, a hope of eternal life, or a belief in something somewhere. It *must* be a *new* life. In 1 John it says:

> If anyone says, 'I love God, and hates his brother, he is a liar; for he who does not love his brother whom he has seen, cannot love God whom he has not seen. 1 John 4: 20 (RSV)

Christian faith can never be an escape from the problems and troubles of this world. Christ was not crucified in some lovely church on the altar between two silver candlesticks. He was crucified between two thieves in the midst of hate, dirt, misunderstanding, and pain. Christian faith is a calling, a transformation, a preparation to deal better with the problems and troubles of this life.

For discussion

1. How would you answer a person who says, 'I am free, I do whatever I like'?
2. Today there are computers that can be programmed to play chess and win every time. But a father, teaching his eight-year-old son to play chess, can also win every time, though sometimes he chooses to lose to encourage his son. Do you think a computer will ever be able to do this?
3. What is the difference between a computer and a father?

10,000 children die of starvation every day

Your faith and your world

Did you know these facts about your fellow-man?

85% live without proper sewage disposal
70% live without clean drinking water
30% live in hovels
60% of all deaths are a result of starvation
10,000 children die each day of starvation

If you have a radio or TV or buy a newspaper then you have the whole world and its problems in your home. The world has become so much smaller during the past fifty years—and it's going to shrink a lot more. Via the mass media you are a part of race riots in Chicago, war in the Middle East, starvation in Bangladesh, or peace negotiations in Geneva. Since the Christian faith, if it is to be alive, must deal with the problems of the world, it must also deal with these problems. It is of course, true that you will most often function as a Christian on the local level among family and friends. This is also the best training ground for Christian living (see Luke 16: 10). But your faith can never stay within your own little circle. The needs, injustices, and tensions of the world cry out for your faith, love, understanding and commitment. The question is *how* can we help?

The problems of the world have become so huge and complicated that if we are to solve them we must do things together. A single individual feels quite helpless. As Christians we must work together with both Christians and non-Christians who also want to create a world of peace, justice, and freedom. There are many local organizations in which we could be active.

There are many active Christians fighting for justice in the world today. Among them are Bishop Dom Helder Camara in Brazil, who is

fighting for the poor of North-eastern Brazil; Ceasar Chavez who organized the grape-pickers of America to fight for better living conditions; and the Rev. Jesse Jackson, who is behind black economic power as an instrument to create a better life for negroes. And there are many, many more.

Perhaps the best-known representative of Christian commitment to justice was the late Dr. Martin Luther King, who won so much for his fellow negroes through non-violent demonstrations, and who was often in prison for this commitment. He was eventually shot.

The church has long been either half-active, inactive or even in opposition to change in our world. The church must not be like this in the future.

But those groups in our society who are actively trying to change things don't need just your support; they need the love, understanding and forgiveness that must be a product of the Christian faith. It is all too easy for an individual to go under in a mass movement and lose responsibility, balance and even reality. Revolutions and mass movements have a very easy time getting off the track. People have a tremendous ability to destroy their finest and highest thoughts and ideals. The history of the church shows this probably more clearly than anything else. History also tells of revolutions which began with great and noble ideals, but which ended up in hate, injustice, and even massacre. There is no church, group, political organization, revolution or idea which is immune to egoism and power-hunger. As Christians we must be active, but also sufficiently honest and courageous to bear responsibility as individuals, and to show love even for our enemies and to have a deep respect for *truth*.

For discussion

1. Do you think Christians should give money to liberation organizations (a) to buy weapons (b) to buy first-aid materials (c) not at all? Explain your choice.
2. 'Christians think only about heaven. They can't be active in world problems.' How would you answer this statement?

People are not things

The Ten Commandments

Once upon a time there was a king who was crazy about gold. He tried in every way to get as much gold as possible. Night and day the only thing he thought about was gold. One day, it occurred to him that it would be wonderful if he had the power to turn to gold everything he touched. The idea left him no peace. Due to some strange event, his wish came true. He had the power to turn things into gold. He walked to the centre of the room and placed his hand on the table. It was immediately turned to 24-carat gold. The table was then so heavy that the floor began to break under it. So the king touched the floor and that too turned into gold. During the next few minutes he changed everything into gold—curtains, chairs, paintings. Everything became gold. He had never in his life experienced so much excitement. Never had any room been so beautiful in his eyes as the gold room now before him.

After a few minutes, the king went to the table again. On the table was a fruit-bowl. He reached out his hand to take an apple. It fell from his fingers, a huge gold nugget. Suddenly fear filled the king. His dream was a nightmare. He would now starve to death. He tried to drink water but that didn't work either. The water changed to gold as soon as he touched it. His dream had become his condemnation—a catastrophe!

Just then the king's daughter came into the room. If there was anything the king loved more than gold it was his twelve-year-old daughter. He began to tell her of his catastrophe and, without thinking, tried to embrace her. And then the worst of all happened! The girl turned into gold.

The king was granted his wish, but lost much much more. He lost his daughter. He had a statue, which was her exact likeness and made of

91

24-carat gold! But how worthless this statue was to him! A statue is only a *thing*—and even if it were a 24-carat *thing*, it was still only a *thing* and not his living daughter.

People are not just *things*: they are so much more. The relationship we have with people is something quite different from the contact we have with *things*. The most wonderful and meaningful things we experience in life happen in relationship with God and with people. This contact or relationship is of unbelievable importance. We can say that it is holy.

Someone has said that the Ten Commandments can be shortened to 'You shall not turn either God, yourself, or your neighbour into *things*.'

The Ten Commandments are meant to *help us*. In a way, they are guide-lines which show us how to live and preserve the relationship we have with God, and with our fellow men. The Ten Commandments are meant to help us *not* to make God and our fellow men into *things* that we use, exploit, or neglect. The Commandments don't exist to make life hard and gloomy for us—quite the reverse! They are meant to help us take care of those things in life which we *know* mean most to us.

For discussion

1. Why was the gold statue worthless to the king?
2. What is the message of this story?

Who has power over whom?

The First Commandment:* **I am the Lord, thy God. Thou shalt have no other gods before me**

Originally, the first Commandment was supposed to forbid people to worship gods which they themselves had made, bought, or inherited; gods, for example, made of stone or wood. Maybe we think that such a Commandment has little to offer modern man. We think that a primitive person who worships 'man-made' gods is quite stupid. But is that person really all that stupid? Don't you think he knows that what he worships is only stone or wood? Perhaps that's why he does it. A god of stone or wood is something that he can own or control, instead of the other way around. He can beg from it, bargain with it, and when it doesn't work any longer, he can break it into pieces. Isn't this exactly what many people do with God? They demand something they can see, something they can touch, something to *prove* that God really exists. When they don't get what they demand, they break to pieces and reject everything that has to do with 'belief in God' and become atheists. There are also those who want to make God into something that can be used, enjoyed, or exploited. But their 'god' comes across more like a Santa Claus than what Christianity understands by God. When these people don't get any presents or dividends from their god, they are finished with religion.

Why do people want to make God into a thing? Because they want to have power over him. But God is not a *thing* that can be used or exploited. We are supposed to love him with all our hearts, minds, strength and souls. As Luther says, we are to 'love and trust in God above all things', just as we 'love and trust' when we fall in love, without demanding absolute proof that we are loved, or without

* Some groups use the listing of the Ten Commandments as they are found in this book and others divide the First Commandment into two, identifying the two, and combine the last two on covetousness into one.

requiring a guarantee that we will be happy for ever. He who asks for proof or a guarantee doesn't understand what love is all about. And he who always wants to make God into a thing and demands proof from him, doesn't understand what belief is all about.

There are, of course, many things in our lives that we make into gods, such as money, jobs, the standard of living, and maybe even the church. But the worst thing is when we make God into a *thing*, instead of a God who loves and whom we are to love. To make God into just a 'higher power', for example, is to do just that. Do we make God into a *thing* because a God who loves is impossible? Or is it because we want to escape a God who reaches into our very hearts and changes our lives?

A name that is holy

The Second Commandment: **Thou shalt not take the name of the Lord thy God in vain**

In Old Testament times a name meant much more than it does today. To use or even write a person's name meant that you had power over him. Our modern 'ad-men' understand how much power a name can have. They try to imprint in us the name of a certain product. If they succeed, then each time we buy a detergent, for example, we don't just think about that detergent, but we think of 'TIDE'.

Many people feel that this Commandment has to do with those times when we swear or drop something and say 'Oh God!' This is probably one of our more innocent ways of misusing the name of God. The worst thing we can do is to misuse the name of God by making the word 'God' into a *thing* that can be used for a specific purpose. For example, many say something like this:

'If God really existed then he would stop war and hatred.'
They use the name 'God' to escape their own responsibility for war and hatred.

Or,

'I swear to God!'
Here we are using the word 'God' to prove to others that we are reliable.

Or,

'. . . And let us not tire or weaken in our struggle against the godless communists!'
Here the word 'God' is being used to increase the hatred against people of a particular political view.

Or,

'. . . We are the people of God doing his will and work!'
Here the name 'God' is used to flatter ourselves. We use it for egotistical purposes.

Or,

'This is a holy war. We are fighting for God!'

Here again we use 'God' to defend our own actions. Is there anything more impossible than a *holy* war?

Jesus says:

Not every one who says to me, Lord, Lord, shall enter the kingdom of heaven, but he who does the will of my Father who is in heaven. On that day many will say to me, Lord, Lord, did we not prophesy in your name, and cast out demons in your name and do many mighty works in your name? And then will I declare to them, I never knew you; depart from me, you evildoers.

Matthew 7: 21–23 (RSV)

We also misuse the name of our Lord when we don't use it at all. It is *supposed to be used* daily, not as a subject of discussion or debate, but as the name of the one to whom you pray and call for help. The name of God must not be misused, but used. Luther doesn't write only about what must *not* be done with God's name but says '. . . call upon him in every time of need, and worship him with prayer, praise and thanksgiving.'

For discussion

1. How do we make God into a 'thing'?
2. What kind of idols do you have?

A day for you

The Third Commandment: **Remember the Sabbath day to keep it holy**

Sunday is our day. It is a day for people, and it is supposed to be a day of rest. You are not supposed to work all the time. Any doctor will tell you that stress isn't good for you and that you must take it easy sometimes and relax. The problem is that our Sundays are often everything but relaxing. In the first place, people try to get as much as possible done on Sundays. They work in their gardens or on their boats, or they are stuck in traffic for several hours. They just don't have time to relax.

Secondly, stress doesn't have to do only with how many hours you work and how tired your muscles are. It has to do with 'the inner person'—the inside of you. Human beings are not machines that can shut down on Friday evening so that they will be rested when Monday comes. Human beings bring their troubles and worries home with them. Thus, for many people, Sunday is not a day of rest, but the most stressful day of the week. Psychologists call this the 'Sunday neurosis'.

A few years ago a study was made, showing that misuse of alcohol during a given week was greatest on Sunday afternoons. How can that be the case? It is because people get along better during their working hours than during their free time. When they are working they don't have much time to think and 'feel'. But during the week-end, all their worries and troubles have time to surface. The solution is not that people should work all the time. They can't take that, and in that way they never really get at the problem. The solution is to get at their troubles and worries. This is the main task of the church in order to help people to discover meaning in their lives, and to show them the forgiveness and fellowship of God. That's why the church has services each Sunday.

Christianity is realistic. Sometimes it hurts to hear what is being preached in church. You don't want to hear that you are a sinner. But that is the truth. It isn't very much fun going to the doctor either. He might tell you that you are sick. But if you really *are* sick, then you had better find out so that you can be helped. That's what doctors are for. And the church doesn't only tell you that you are a sinner. In church you also receive peace, forgiveness and guidance. In church you are to experience joy. That's what the word 'gospel' means: 'the message of joy or good news.'

You feel joy because God has done something—something that touches man in his heart, that gives him peace and which equips him to serve his fellow man.

You and I are very clever at swindling ourselves and being dishonest with ourselves. We need to go to church. We need to go there often.

For discussion

1. How do you suffer from 'Sunday neurosis'?
2. Why is there often a *confession of sins* in church services? Is it to punish people?
3. Someone says to you: 'I don't need to go to church. I have my worship service in God's nature.' If you wanted to know if this person *really* had a service in nature, what would you ask him?

Your nearest neighbour

The Fourth Commandment: **Honour thy father and thy mother that thy days may be long upon the land which the Lord thy God giveth thee**

When I was a child I misunderstood the fourth Commandment completely. I thought it read like this: 'Honour thy father and thy mother that *their* days may be long. . . .' When I realized that I had it all wrong, I had a hard time understanding what it was really supposed to mean. But after having read the following story by the Brothers Grimm I understood.

Once upon a time there was a little old man. He was blind and his hands trembled. When he ate he made a terrible noise with his silverware. He missed his mouth with his spoon just as often as he found it and dropped food on the tablecloth. The man lived together with his son who was married to a young modern woman who felt that parents-in-law should not live in the same house as their children.

'I just can't go on like this,' she said. 'This is an intrusion into my right to happiness.'

She and her husband took the little man by the arm and put him down on a stool in a corner of the kitchen. There he ate his food from a clay bowl. When it was mealtime he always sat there, looking with blind but sad and longing eyes towards the table.

One day his hands trembled more than usual and the bowl of clay fell to the floor and broke.

'If you are a pig,' said his daughter-in-law, 'then you must eat from a bucket.'

So they made a wooden bucket for him from which he ate his food.

It so happened that this couple had a son who was four years old. They were very fond of him. One day after supper the young man

101

noticed that his little boy was busy playing with some pieces of wood and he asked the boy what he was doing.

'I'm making a wooden bucket,' said the boy with a big smile, 'so that I can feed you and mummy from it, when I grow up.'

The man and his wife looked at each other for a while but didn't say anything. They couldn't help crying a little. But then they went over to the corner, took the old man by the arm and brought him back to the table. They put him in a comfortable chair and gave him food on a plate. Never again did they say anything if he dropped or broke things.

When you are in your youth, your relationship with your parents is radically changed. Of course, you would like this change to be to your advantage. You are going to be free—you are going to grow up. But what does it mean to grow up? It means that *you* are responsibe instead of your mother or father. But it means even more. To grow up means that you discover your parents in a new way, not just as parents, but also as your very closest fellow men—your nearest neighbours. You will discover that your mother and father often make big mistakes, just as you do. You will find that sometimes they are afraid and lonely, and that they need love, forgiveness and meaning in their lives—just as you do. You will discover that being grown-up is pretty rough. It doesn't only mean that now you can get a driver's licence, buy a drink and go to adult movies. Your parents don't have an easy time. Their jobs are often tiring and cause stress. They have a great responsibility to their family. Your mother often experiences her job as a housewife boring and meaningless.

You are grown up when you stop just asking and receiving from your parents and start giving instead. They need your love, your understanding and your patience more than you will ever realize or they admit. And remember the story above! When you have children of your own they'll learn how to treat their parents by watching how you treat yours.

For discussion

1. What is the message of the story of Brothers Grimm?
2. Someday your fifteen-year-old daughter says to you: 'It's my life not yours. I am the one who decides not you. My life is none of your business!' What would you answer her?

There are many ways to kill

The Fifth Commandment: **Thou shalt not kill**

At first glance this Commandment seems simple to understand and to follow. 'Most people aren't murderers, are they?' someone says. Aren't we? Aren't most of us guilty because we haven't lived according to this commandment, even though we haven't shot anyone? Jesus says:

You have heard that it was said to the men of old, 'You shall not kill; and whoever kills shall be liable to judgment.' But I say to you that every one who is angry with his brother shall be liable to judgment; whoever insults his brother shall be liable to the council, and whoever says, You fool! shall be liable to the hell of fire.

Matthew 5: 21–22 (RSV)

A human being isn't just a body—a thing. A human being is 'feelings', heart and soul. You can kill people inside, in their feelings or hearts. Think how often we hurt those nearest to us, not with weapons but with words, glances and thoughts. Think how often we have the opportunity to help with a word, with friendliness, with even a glance, but we keep quiet: we close our eyes to it. Just simply saying, 'I'm sorry' can often bring to life a person who is 'dead' inside. That's why forgiveness is so absolutely essential.

When we begin considering the inner lives and feelings of people, then we've come a big step closer to peace between countries and individuals, and between you and your fellow men.

To kill doesn't just mean to murder someone. We can also kill by refusing to help someone who needs our help to survive. Luther says: 'We should fear and love God so that we do our neighbour no bodily harm nor cause him any suffering, *but help and befriend him in every need*.' The world is full of people who are suffering and are in danger. What are you doing to, '. . . help and befriend him in every need'? In the story of the Good Samaritan the thieves aren't the only 'sinners' because they are guilty of having wounded a person; the priest and the Levite are guilty also because they pass by on the other side.

Drive Carefully

One day, you are driving through a densely populated area. You like the feeling of having the wheel in your hands and so much horsepower at your command. It's so easy to increase the speed, and so you do just that. Suddenly a ball rolls out between two parked cars. You suspect danger ahead. You move your foot to the brake pedal. Suddenly a little boy runs out after the ball, right in front of your car. You brake hard but you are going too fast. You hear a terrible noise—a noise you will never forget. You rush out of the car and run to the boy. He doesn't move. He is dead. You must notify his parents. But what are you going to say? Of course the boy shouldn't have run out into the street like that but.... Of course he should have looked but.... Is there any sum of money on this earth that can replace what the little boy meant to his parents? DRIVE CAREFULLY! You can't *replace a person*!

Defence and War

How do defence and war relate to the fifth Commandment? Christians can honestly have different opinions about these things. Many feel that war and preparations for war contradict all that Jesus taught and all that has to do with loving your neighbour. There is a great deal of truth in what they say. Many people feel that sometimes it is necessary to fight a war in order to save the lives of others. A pastor in Germany, Dietrich Bonhoeffer, was executed in 1945 because he was involved in an attempt on Hitler's life on the 20th July, 1944. Many people were shocked that a pastor would involve himself in anything like that. But Bonhoeffer felt that you don't only have a responsibility to those who have been run over by some careless driver, but you also have a responsibility to stop the fool behind the wheel.

Some people feel that the best protection against war is a strong defence. They mean by this that a strong defence makes an attack too 'expensive' for the attacker.

Others have a different opinion and feel that a strong defence hasn't stopped war before, so why should it be able to do it now. They feel that the best way to keep peace in the world is to put more money—a great deal of the money that now is spent on defence—into the under-developed countries, so that the gap between the rich and the poor countries will be made smaller and one of the causes of war will be eliminated.

On the one hand you might feel that of course you have to have defence. There always has been defence because you can't safely be without it, can you?

On the other hand, you might say: 'Why not?—doesn't Christian love mean that you make yourself vulnerable or defenceless, as Christ made himself defenceless for our sake? Isn't it about time that we seriously *try* another way?' We know that the old way hasn't worked in this world. We won't get closer to each other by frightening and threatening each other with what *every* country calls 'defence'.

Young people today will deal with these questions to a greater extent than any other generation has ever done before. These are hard, deep and painful questions that demand honesty with ourselves, and love and understanding for others.

For discussion

1. Did Dietrich Bonhoeffer do the right thing?
2. Should Christians bear arms?
3. How can we 'wage' peace?

You need faithfulness

The Sixth Commandment: **Thou shalt not commit adultery**

People are strange. Although they don't want to be alone and even though they need each other so much, they still have a very difficult time in getting really close to one another. They want their freedom, even though love demands that they give it up. They want to be very close to another person, but at the same time, not too close. John Steinbeck once expressed the problem like this: 'We are afraid of being alone and we are afraid of being together.'

To share your life and your deepest feelings with another human being demands a great deal of trust. We would like to expand our trust and make it stronger. We would like to share our life with another person. But do we dare?

The greatest aid we have in creating trust in one another is love. Not just the exciting feeling of falling in love. Love is a demanding and often a painful *giving* of yourself, your life and your feelings to another person. Sexual relationships are a means by which we can express this trust and love in a very wonderful way. Sex is something tangible and real. As such it can function as the most beautiful expression of a love that binds two people together. Christianity has a deep understanding of how important it is for two people to give themselves to each other in total trust and love. The church wants to guard the value of sex because it really *is* something. It is something great, rich and meaningful.

There are, however, few things today more able than sex to turn people into 'things'. *People are not things that we use*! But we make people into things, when, for example, we make girls into 'pin-ups'. Just think what a tragedy it is for a girl to discover that she is *only* beautiful! What a blow to her to discover that the interest the opposite sex has shown in her has not been in her as a *person*, because she was *she*, but because she was a 'thing'. She was a 'picture' of what boys are

106

supposed to think is nice looking. Why be only a body when you can be a whole person? That people become 'things' happens even *within* marriage. It happens when people commit a different kind of adultery from what most people mean by this word. Wives or husbands can be *used* as a *means of pleasure* instead of being *experienced* as persons with feelings and needs of love and trust. This happens when people get married without ever *really* entering into marriage on its deepest and most personal level.

If sex is so important, so filled with feeling, so essential as an expression of love and trust, then you can't be unfaithful without hurting your relationship. People sometimes say: 'It doesn't make any difference if you are unfaithful as long as she or he doesn't find out about it.' But is this true? *You* know about it. You know that you *haven't kept* the trust that love demands.

We live in a time of rapid and far-reaching change. One wonders if we will have time to get used to the new before the next change comes. Attitudes and opinions about sex have really been shaken up by the changes of our time. Puberty is reached earlier, more time is spent in school, and there is a mass mobility of people from the country to big cities. People have easy access to contraceptives. All this has left its mark on and changed the way people look upon sex. The whole role of sex is being questioned. Norms have been challenged and many will be changed. During this process of change we must be on our guard so that that which is valuable will not be destroyed.

Free morals

There is today a very active minority that preaches freedom from moral rules and norms. Free morality is a flight from reality—there is no such thing. We don't take away morality and norms: we only change them and exchange them. The question is whether the new morality or new norms function better or worse than those that they are supposed to replace. Many say that the norm which restricts sexual relations to marriage, should disappear because it creates guilt-feelings in those who have premarital relationships. But the opposite may also cause a kind of guilt-feeling. If the new norm permits premarital relationships, it may create guilt-feelings in those who don't have the opportunity for them, and who therefore look upon themselves as some kind of misfit.

The question is, where should the limits be? When should sexual relationships start? Many feel that they can start as soon as they are

'in love'. But what is 'in love'? How do you know if you are really in love, or only experiencing a crush?

Pornography

Lately pornographic books and magazines have been published in greater quantities than ever before. Pornography has grown into an 'industry' where people have made lots of money. The problem with pornography is that it is so very unreal. It often describes sexual drives and behaviour that are not only unrealistic, but also totally impossible. What makes pornography dangerous is that people who read it may form a picture of sex that is quite unreal. If you get married with the outlook on sex that you get from pornography you are going to have problems. People just aren't like that. The danger is that you will look upon yourself and your husband or wife as abnormal compared to what you've read and seen in pornographic material. *You* are not abnormal: pornography is!

For discussion

1. William H. Masters, a leading expert on sexual problems, said once, 'The best form of sexual education is when dad walks past mum in the kitchen and pats her on the rear and she enjoys it. The child sees this and thinks, "That's for me".' What do you think he meant?
2. Someone said, 'Sex isn't something you do, it is something you are.' What does this mean? Does it mean that one should be sexy?
3. What does it mean 'to be in love'?

Little thieves and big thieves

The Seventh Commandment: **Thou shalt not steal**

You go up to your room to play one of your favourite records—but you can't find it. Strange, you are sure that it was there yesterday. The same evening you go to a friend's house. In his collection of records you find just the record you had been looking for earlier in the day! Charlie was at your house yesterday. When you answered the telephone he disappeared. Now you know why. He notices that you are looking at the record and knows that certain thoughts are going through your head. He tells you that his father bought him the record last week. But you *know* that it is yours, because you recognize a scratch on the cover. You don't say anything. But you don't stay very long either. How do you feel when you go home? You are angry. But more than that, you are disappointed. What hurts most is not that you've lost a record but that you've lost a friend. Charlie obviously places greater value on a stupid record than on your friendship. From now on your relationship will not be the same. Even if you hadn't discovered that Charlie had stolen from you, things would not now be the same. *Charlie* knows that he has stolen from you and would have avoided you in the future, anyway. He didn't care about your friendship, nor your feelings. He *used* you to get a record.

There are few things that destroy relationships between people as theft does. A person's money and belongings are not ordinary things. They are part of a person's life. Someone has said that 'money is congealed time, sweat and thoughts'. Money is the part of your life that you've exchanged for cash. To take someone's money or belongings is the same as taking a part of him. To steal is to use or exploit your fellow men. You can steal in many ways without breaking into someone's house and without using violence. You can cheat in an exam and steal information and results that don't belong to you. You can be dishonest

when you make out your tax return, and you can steal from everyone. You can refuse to pay your employees a just salary and in this way use and exploit them. You can steal by demanding more wages than you actually deserve.

Today, the most cruel way of stealing is when we don't give enough help to the poor of the world so as to make their lives at least tolerable.

Not long ago many thought that the poor or underdeveloped countries would catch up with the industrialized countries and the gap between the rich and the poor countries would disappear. Unfortunately this has turned out to be but a dream. The industrialized countries get richer and richer and the poor countries at best stand still, and at worst, get poorer. With population increases, lack of money and technology, the poor countries must run very fast just to keep the standard they now have. If this trend continues, and all signs say it will, then this will mean that the underdeveloped countries become more and more dependent on us (read here, 'be under our control'). Since we have the economical and technological might, we will always be able to force them to take a smaller share of what they produce and sell than what they ought to receive. This is theft! We may create lovely explanations for our crimes. But, it is theft whatever you call it. How are you going to solve this problem?

Recently we have discovered yet another way in which we are guilty of theft. We have found out that we are guilty of stealing from the next generation, from our children and grandchildren. We steal from them every time one of our lakes is destroyed by pollution. It is also theft when we poison the air we breathe. If we don't stop polluting nature, future generations will live in a world that is much more impoverished than the world we have today. God did not create it like this. It is being destroyed because we are such poor stewards of the creation God has placed in our hands.

For discussion

1. Someone says to you: 'Don't steal from me because then you will avoid me and we need each other.' What does this mean?
2. Seen from space the world has no borders. Why are they there?
3. Why are there rich and poor countries?
4. 'We have met the enemy—and it is us!' What does this mean?

When truth suffers

The Eighth Commandment: **Thou shalt not bear false witness against thy neighbour**

At some time or another we have all experienced how a truth, half-truth or a lie has circulated among friends or acquaintances and how changed and twisted everything has become. It seems as if people find some kind of pleasure in enlarging and twisting things they hear to make them worse than they are. Why do we like to put the worst interpretation on things? Isn't this also a way of using people? We can *use* people as exciting topics of conversation. We can also use people's problems and mistakes so that we can have an excuse for not having anything to do with them. This way we can avoid loving and helping them. We can also in this way make these people into a kind of dark and shady background against which we stand out in contrast as better people than they. Here again we make people into things that we use and exploit for our own benefit. We don't care if people get hurt, angry, sad or even crushed. This is something we must watch out for. Gossip is habit-forming. It becomes automatic. Some people go so far that bearing false witness becomes a life-style for them. These people end up being very lonely and bitter.

Bearing false witness against your neighbour has become a big part of both local and international politics. Someone once said that if phrases didn't exist, neither would war. Every day, false and half-true rumours are spread about our neighbours in other countries, about other nationalities, and political camps.

To seek and to support truth is a heavy and often painful task. It means that you must study, question, examine, analyse, and dare to have your own opinion about things. It's easy to yell propaganda and clichés. It just takes a few seconds. But to seek the truth is a life-long struggle.

'Don't lie, it's too much work?' What does this mean?

Two commandments for our thoughts

The Ninth Commandment: **Thou shalt not covet thy neighbour's house**

The Tenth Commandment: **Thou shalt not covet thy neighbour's wife, nor his manservant, nor his maidservant, nor his cattle, nor anything that is thy neighbour's**

The first eight Commandments have to do with our outward actions. The last two Commandments have to do with our thoughts and feelings. It is essential that the commandments concern even this area for, as we have seen, most of the problems of the world start in our hearts. These two commandments are based on the weakness people have for treating their fellow men according to what they *have* or *own*, instead of according to what *they are*.

Notice that the commandment does not say that *to desire* something is wrong in itself. What is wrong is to desire something *that belongs to someone else*. This is to *covet*. When a man desires a woman it invariably leads to love and marriage. When a man desires his *neighbour's wife* it can lead to adultery. If the inhabitants of a country desire more land for agriculture, this can lead to better use of the land they possess. It can lead to irrigation of deserts, drainage of swamps, etc. But if they desire the land of their neighbours, it can lead to war.

For discussion

Think through the difference between 'to covet' something and 'to desire' something. Find other illustrations.

The 'eleventh' commandment

> Then a certain teacher of the Law came up and tried to trap Jesus.
> 'Teacher,' he asked, 'What must I do to receive eternal life?' Jesus
> answered him, 'What do the Scriptures say? How do you interpret
> them?' The man answered, 'You must love the Lord your God
> with all your heart, and with all your soul, and with all your
> strength, and with all your mind'; and, 'You must love your
> neighbour as yourself.' 'Your answer is correct,' replied Jesus;
> 'do this and you will live.'
>
> Luke 10: 25–28 (Good News for Modern Man)

This Commandment is sometimes referred to as the eleventh Commandment and is often considered to be an abbreviation of the Ten Commandments. What is meant by this is that if you live according to this commandment then you will not break the other commandments. This may be true but that doesn't in any way mean it is easier to live according to this eleventh Commandment.

I have often heard people say that the second half of this commandment that says that we are to love our neighbour as ourselves, is the most important part. There is truth here of course. But do people really love their neighbours as themselves? Can you really 'love your neighbour as yourself', without a very radical change and reorientation within yourself? I doubt it. Such a change does take place however when you 'love the Lord your God with all your heart, and with all your soul, and with all your strength, and with all your mind'.

This kind of love encompasses a person's whole way of thinking, seeing, hearing and being. On the other hand if you don't love your neighbour then no change has taken place and you have not loved God.

What does 'as yourself' mean? Some people wonder if this isn't just another expression of egoism. But this is not what is meant. It does *not* mean that you should love your neighbour as 'you are in love with yourself. It means that you are to place the same value on your neighbour as you place on yourself—and just as naturally and spontaneously.

In Luke 10: 29–37 we find one of the best descriptions of a natural and spontaneous love. It is here that Jesus tells the story of the Good Samaritan as an answer to the teacher of the law who asked him, 'Who is my neighbour?'

When the Good Samaritan comes up to the man lying in the road, he doesn't see a man of a particular race, nationality or political opinion. He sees a fellow human being *in need* and helps him, just as spontaneously and naturally as if he himself had been lying there half dead. The gospel of Luke does not say that he gave this help because it was his duty to do so, or because the law said he should. He *reacted* spontaneously from his goodness and love for his fellow man.

Rules and laws are necessary to keep order in society and to give guidance on what is right and wrong. But they cannot *force* goodness or love between men. These things must come spontaneously and naturally, from within. If you yourself happen to hurt your arm, you run for help, immediately, without first reflecting whether the arm that is hurt belongs to a black man, a white man or a yellow man. You react without considering what political opinion the owner of the arm has. This is obvious when it concerns yourself. To love your neighbour as yourself means to help him just as spontaneously.

For discussion

Work out the meaning of 'as yourself' in this eleventh commandment. Give specific examples.

Two great gifts for you

The Protestant church has two great gifts from God. Some people call them sacraments; others call them ordinances. These gifts are given through baptism and communion. In baptism we receive God's promise of love, care, and forgiveness. In communion we experience God's presence, love and forgiveness through bread and wine. This does *not*, of course, mean that God's love, forgiveness and presence do not exist apart from the sacraments. The purpose of a sacrament is to make these things living, real and personal to us. You know how important it is to you that those who love you show you their love by their actions as well as by their words. It can mean a great deal to you if you become a part of what God will give you through his sacraments.

Baptism

Jesus said to his disciples:

> All authority in heaven and on earth has been given to me. Go therefore and make disciples of all nations, baptizing them in the name of the Father and of the Son and of the Holy Spirit, teaching them to observe all that I have commanded you; and lo, I am with you always, to the close of the age.
>
> Matthew 28: 18–20 (RSV)

Many people are baptized when they are babies and don't remember anything of their baptism. Many others believe that it is wrong to baptize babies since they don't understand what is happening. But baptism doesn't deal with what we understand but with what God promises us and will give us. I am sure that I will never 'understand' God's forgiveness nor his power but I can become a part of it and experience it.

It is the responsibility of the church and of parents to teach children what it means to belong to God's kingdom and to be a part of his love and power. This is one of the reasons why parents and the church want their children to learn the meaning of the Christian faith. In those churches where babies are baptized, there are usually confirmation classes. Confirmation means that after instruction, honest searching and prayer you say 'Yes, I would like to continue living in God's kingdom and his church as I have since I was baptized.' In those churches where babies are not baptized, young people and adults are baptized after they have expressed their own commitment to Christ and the church. Usually they receive instruction in the meaning of the Christian faith and church membership before they are baptized. As children they have usually shared in the experience of the Christian community, and now, at their baptism, they declare their intention to become responsible members of that community.

Holy Communion

> ... The Lord Jesus on the night when he was betrayed took bread, and when he had given thanks, he broke it, and said, This is my body which is for you. Do this in remembrance of me. In the same way also the cup, after supper, saying, This cup is the new covenant in my blood. Do this, as often as you drink it, in remembrane of me.   1 Cor. 11: 23–25 (RSV)

When we take holy communion we join with Christ, as did Jesus' disciples on the night when he was betrayed. It was this first communion that the disciples found so impossible to understand.

While each individual takes communion, communion is never a solitary experience. We share with other Christians whether we pass the communion from one to another in the pew or gather at the altar rail. Not only do we experience a fellowship with those who are around us, but we are part of a much larger fellowship as well. In those churches where the altar ring forms a half-circle, the wider fellowship can easily be imagined. The unseen part of the circle is made up of those who have come to holy communion throughout history. The unseen section is the 'communion of saints' spoken of in the Creed. It is within this great fellowship of faith that the church of Christ celebrates holy communion.

But communion is not only an experience of fellowship with other believers. It is also a celebration of remembrance of what Christ has done for us through his suffering and death. It is also a confession that we have hurt others, created chaos instead of harmony, and it is a confession of faith in the forgiveness and peace of God that is ours in holy communion. It is with freedom, joy and thanksgiving, that we leave the Lord's table and retake our places in a world in need of precisely what communion offers us.

Many ask: 'Who is worthy to take communion?' Those who ask this have not understood either communion or Christianity. Communion and Christianity are for the unworthy—for sinners. If you are honest with yourself and your sins, then you should take communion. He who is worthy to take communion is he who admits that he is unworthy.

How often should a person take communion? You should take communion when you know that you have hurt other people, when you see that you have been blind to other people's needs and feelings, when you, by your selfishness, destroy your possibilities to love, forgive and create peace, when you are worried and in need of the peace of God, when you doubt and have a hard time believing, when you feel the need of fellowship with Jesus and his disciples both present and past. *You need communion and you need it often.*

For discussion

1. Which of the following statements do you accept and which do you reject? Give your reasons.
   (a) Babies should be baptized,
   (b) only babies whose parents are willing to raise them as Christians should be bapitzed,
   (c) only adults should be baptized.
2. Read 1 Corinthians 11: 23–25. What does Jesus mean by what he says about the bread and the wine?
3. In what way are the meaning of baptism and the meaning of communion alike and in what way different?
4. Do you need communion?